UNCONVENTIONAL BUILDERS

UNCONVENTIONAL BUILDERS

by Alan Van Dine

Design by Ron Villani

Holly Harrington   Picture Editor

J. G. Ferguson Publishing Company, Chicago

Jacket photo credits:
Jericho — Historical Pictures Service, Chicago
Hausa Dwellings — Deane Rawson from Photo Researchers

Copyright © 1977 by J. G. Ferguson Publishing Company
International Standard Book Number: 0-89434-001-8
Library of Congress Catalog Card Number: 76-445-87

Dedicated to clever men
like Christopher Wren
Beowulf
Shakespeare
Joshua
Ch'in
Louis XIV
Incas
Eskimos
Irish monks
Neanderthals
ghosts
and clever birds
like the Least Bittern

TABLE OF CONTENT

PREFACE

The year Benjamin Franklin was born, a six-inch tooth was unearthed in Massachusetts. In those dim pre-Darwin, pre-paleontology days, the discovery seemed sufficiently ominous that the tooth was promptly brought before the Governor of the colony. Lacking certain essential points of evidence — for example, that mastodons ever existed — the Governor announced that the tooth belonged to a giant man who had been drowned in the Great Flood.

It is never easy to take a piece from the past and imagine its owner, its context, or its reason for being. When the remnants are the largest artifacts of man — his buildings — the imagining is easier but sometimes just as wild. And given the intensity of human hope, ambition, fear, greed, pride, or reverence necessary to prompt such an arduous project as the raising of a building, wild imaginings are often in order:

A terrified widow appeases the ghosts she fears by building them a 700-room house.

An emperor becomes so obsessed with national defense that he sets out to build a wall around his country.

To hide from predatory Vikings, Irish monks build a refuge tower visible for miles.

A city, bankrupt and starving after a ten-year siege, pours most of its marketable metals into construction of the largest, most extravagant statue on earth.

A small French town races to build the highest spire in history — so high and so hastily built that it cannot stand up.

An otherwise masterful politician commits political suicide by building himself a house that is better than the King's.

The pilgrim wades ashore at Jamestown and builds what? A log cabin? No, a wigwam, and then a medieval English cottage.

The record is not always clear as to why people build the things they do, in the way they do. Ireland's peculiar Round Towers stood in place so long that people in the surrounding countryside entirely forgot why or how the towers first appeared. After a thousand years, even direct descendants of the occupants and builders could be convinced that the towers had been erected in ancient times by visiting Carthaginians, Phoenicians, or Egyptians.

The Vikings, whose pillaging had prompted Irish Monks to build those towers in self-defense, left some architectural mysteries of their own. Why, for example, did these rough-cut, roving warriors trouble to shape the walls of their longhouses into sweeping, convex curves? There were clues in the sophisticated joinery of Viking structures. Though erratic as architects, the Norsemen were masterful shipbuilders. Some of their houses and halls had roofs that looked suspiciously like boats turned upside down, and the walls might simply have followed the boat-hull curvature of the roofing edge.

With a few exceptions the stories in this book have to do with structures rather far removed from the familiar monuments and the well-worn paths of tour guides and architectural texts. Libraries may bulge with explications of Shakespeare's plays, but his Globe Theater remains a mystery: no building, no ruins, no plans, no eyewitness descriptions have been seen for over three hundred years. The Tower of Babel has vanished, as has Heorot, the fabled mead hall where Beowulf struggled with Grendel. The log cabin is well known but widely misunderstood, thanks to the ballyhoo of two nineteenth-century presidential elections. Pizarro wrecked the Inca monuments. Louis XIV sacked the magnificent chateau Vaux le Viconte in order to embellish Versailles. And gravity felled the incredible spire of Beauvais Cathedral.

Any modern account of structures such as these—and the high hopes they once carried aloft—must begin with ruins and proceed through legend to what can reasonably be regarded as fact. In most cases scholars have sifted the evidence with more shrewdness and a great deal more data than the Governor could muster when presented with the remains of a mastodon. Each chapter in this book is indebted to researchers too numerous to credit who have done the real work of compiling fact and theory.

These narratives were commissioned by Koppers Company, Inc. and first appeared in a series called Tangents—a series of discussions for the building design professions, published by Koppers and recommended by them as non-urgent reading for architects and engineers. They are presented here for anyone who has ever stared at an odd-looking building and wondered why on earth anyone would want to build *that*.

Clever men
Like Christopher Wren
Only occur just now and then[1]

SIR CHRISTOPHER WREN

It has been said of Christopher Wren that never in his ninety-one years was he ever heard to express himself profanely. If that can be believed—that a man can practice architecture for more than half a century; can deal with five English monarchs, dozens of high officials of church and state, scores of committees and commissions, and hundreds of tradesmen and contractors; can settle thousands of questions of design, engineering, costs, and timetables; and can do it all without a single burst of profanity— well, if it can be said of anyone, it can probably be said of Christopher Wren.

1. from verses by Hugh Chesterman, *Kings and Other Things*, Methuen, London

The dome of St. Paul's Cathedral, clearly visible through the smoke and flames, stands majestically defiant during a World War II firebomb raid. Although a large part of the City of London was destroyed in the fire, the cathedral miraculously escaped severe damage.

Sir Christopher Wren is portrayed against the backdrop of one of his greatest achievements, the reconstruction of St. Paul's Cathedral. One of England's most admired architects, Wren was also known for his accomplishments in the fields of geometry and astronomy.

St. Paul's Cathedral was rebuilt after the old structure was destroyed in the Great Fire of London in 1666. The reconstruction, designed by Wren, has become one of the finest architectural landmarks in England.

Radio Times Hulton Picture Library

Radio Times Hulton Picture Library

In speech and manner, he was by all accounts the most gentle of men. He had no taste for polemic, no penchant for assertion and rejoinder. The statements of Christopher Wren exist mainly in stone, in and about the precincts of London. His pen, though it seldom stopped for long, was reserved chiefly for his drawings and for the matter-of-fact correspondence necessary to see that the designs became buildings.

Words, after all, were not his primary medium. He had far more eloquent language at his command. Where exasperation might overtake others, Wren simply proceeded with the work at hand. His ideas were so compelling that they usually prevailed; when they were challenged, he would patiently explain his thinking. When even that did not carry the day, Wren would quietly *build* his arguments rather than continue to debate them. Anticipating

Pitkin Pictorials, Ltd.

The enormous dome dominates both the exterior and interior of St. Paul's Cathedral. The inner dome is painted with frescoes and is surrounded by windows. The grand proportions of the dome lend to the airy spaciousness below.

hard-core resistance to his idea for the great dome of St. Paul's, he calmly executed the same idea on a smaller scale in advance, at St. Stephen's, Walbrook. When decisions went against him, he would redesign, submit an acceptable compromise, and then later begin to make revisions that would restore much of his original plan. One controversy that went against Wren did evoke a touch of sarcasm — but even that was expressed in stone, and his irony proved so subtle that it was 250 years before anyone got the joke.

The occasion was Wren's election to Parliament in 1688, a compliment that he chose to repay by building a handsome town hall for the citizens of New Westminster. It was an excellent arrangement, a ground-floor arcade for the town offices and a large meeting room above. Everyone was happy except the mayor, who feared that the upstairs room was not adequately supported. Despite Wren's consummate mastery of mathematics, physics, and engineering, and despite his reassurances, the mayor continued to worry and finally convinced his official family that two more columns were needed to ensure their safety.

Wren the politician finally acceded to what Wren the architect knew to be redundant clutter. But he had the last word. Two and a half centuries later, workmen on high scaffolding saw what the mayor could not see from the floor: the two afterthought pillars rise almost—but not quite—to the ceiling. Two stately columns—neither touching the ceiling they were supposed to uphold—stand as satirical essays on the foibles of committee design.

Of course, in his day-to-day dealings not all of Sir Christopher's comments were so silent or so subtle. No architect completes seventy major buildings without some recourse to the ancient arts of presenting and explaining. Budgets must be coaxed into being; ruinous suggestions for "improvement" of a design must be neutralized; old habits of thought must be loosened soothingly or appeased with words before they are wrenched from their moorings by the massive audacity of some bold new structural form.

As the letters excerpted here show, Christopher Wren could soothe and appease. He could explain, lecture, teach, and persuade. Far from being tongue-tied, he was a man of letters who could, among other things (among *many* other things), express himself lucidly in English and in Latin. He was of the age of the experimental philosophers, in the tradition of Sir Francis Bacon and the notion of the Renaissance Man—a scholar adept in every important area of human thought and art. And he was a genius.

He made fundamental contributions to astronomy, geometry, physics, even physiology. (He was the first to inject fluids directly into the bloodstream of an animal under laboratory conditions—opium, as it happened, in the vein

Thomas Photos, Oxford

Wren was invited to design his first buildings at Oxford as a great mind rather than a noted architect. The choice proved to be a wise one. University ceremonies are still performed in the Sheldonian Theatre, which was constructed in 1662.

of a dog who, sure enough, became sleepy.) He prepared a definitive treatise on spherical trigonometry. He advanced astronomy with studies of the rings of Saturn and the moons of Jupiter, and with the design of instruments for observation. His inventions and theories—many of them since lost—included an elaborate weather clock, a device for writing in the dark, various musical instruments, a weaving machine, "divers new engines for raising of water," a method "for staying long under water," and another "to measure the Bass and Height of a Mountain only by journeying over it."

When he was invited to design his first buildings—including the Sheldonian Theatre at Oxford—it was not because he had formal training in architecture but because he had become known as one of the best minds in England. However, it was finally architecture that seemed to satisfy him. Once he began its practice, in his thirties, it became his life work,

and he was soon the preeminent architect in England as well as the surveyor general, official architect for all projects under royal control.

Wren's importance and some of his exploits have nourished a popular conception of him as the aloof genius: the man who could majestically redesign all of fire-ravaged London before its ruins stopped smouldering (which he did) and who could later dismiss the demands of the world (which he didn't) with the oft-quoted:

"If anyone calls,
I'm designing St. Paul's."[2]

His actual days, as he lived them, were closer to earth and right in the thick of things. What the surviving records show is that designing buildings in the seventeenth century involved not only the same satisfactions but also the same day-in, day-out frustrations and reversals that every architect has wrestled with ever since—whether or not the architect is a su-

2. This quote, often attributed to Wren, actually comes from a piece of doggerel written about him by Edmund Clerihew Bentley:
Sir Christopher Wren
Said "I am going to dine with some men.
If anybody calls
Say I am designing St. Paul's"

preme genius, and whether or not the client wears a crown.

Inklings of this are evident in some of Wren's correspondence, though only a small fraction of his notes and letters has been preserved. Fortunately there is one surviving series that tracks a design and construction project more or less from start to finish.

These letters are from Wren to Dr. John Fell, Anglican bishop and dean of Christ Church College at Oxford. Christ Church had the largest quadrangle in all of Oxford, thanks largely to the unceasing construction activity a century earlier under its founder, Cardinal Wolsey. Bishop Fell wished to finish what Wolsey had begun, and the notable piece of unfinished business was the main gate to the quadrangle. It had no gate tower, no proper house for Great Tom, the huge bell dedicated to St. Thomas of Canterbury and given to the college after its

removal from Osney Abbey. Determined to build the tower, the Dean called on Christopher Wren at Wren's home in Scotland Yard.

Sir Christopher's first letter on the subject followed soon after.

My Lord

In pursuance of your Comandes I send your Lordship by Moores Coach my worke these Holydayes. I resolved it ought to be Gothick to agree with the Founders worke, yet I have not continued soe busy as he began. It is not a picture I send you nor an imperfect Essay but a designe well studied as to all the Bearing & fit to instruct the Workman if he will study the other Designe of the Groundplot, which at first sight seems perplext, but he will find every necessary Line of several different plans (as the worke varies in rising) shewing how they beare upon one another, compare it with the orthography & the compasses will distinguish which is which plainer then words can express it.

16

The letter goes on to explain how Wren has resolved the structural problems of tying in the new tower to the older stonework and of supporting a square tower on an oblong gatehouse. He then suggests:

Send me the rates & prices of Heddington, Burford Stone, Lime, with water & land carriages I can guesse what is fit to allowe for workemanship, & I will send Your Lordship a perfect estimate of the Charges, upon which you may contract to have it well and securely performed by X'Mas twelve-month.

He asks that his design be returned with the prices since there was only one copy but recommends that Bishop Fell have copies made for use in persuading potential contributors.

A point of concern for Wren at this stage is the likely quality of skilled labor the bishop will be able to obtain. "I cannot boast of Oxford Artists," Wren writes, "though they have a good opinion of themselves." His misgivings soon prove to be well founded.

The first letter is dated May 26, 1681. Two weeks later trouble is already brewing, as Wren discovers the bishop's workmen have begun to lay foundation stones without waiting for the plan. The architect's letter of June 11 begins:

The Designes (which I have not yet) shall not come sooner to my hands than Your Lordship shall have an estimate made and sent by the next post that followes, & I am heartily sorry the foundations are begun without that due consideration which is requisite, soe that (unlesse you take them up again) I am out of all hope this designe will succeed. I am most certain it will not be without unexcusable flawes & cracks & weaknesse in the fabrick when the whole weight comes on, let your workemen warrant what they will.

17

With the construction of the unfinished gateway, the Christ Church College quadrangle was complete. Built in the sixteenth century, the lower portion of the entrance displayed ornamental Gothic style. While incorporating some of the Gothic ornamentation, Wren introduced plain surfaces and bold horizontal lines into the final design of the main gate.

Radio Times Hulton Picture Library

After a patient explanation of how the foundation is to be revamped, using "the trew waies," Wren concludes:

My Lord these & some other thinges in the consequence of the worke which are not provided but essential to the well performance, makes me jealous that your workmen beginning soe giddily will proceed accordingly & that you will find it too late, that every workeman is not fit for a great undertaking only because he is honest. My Lord if the foundations be only layd of Burres, I again entreat they be taken up, & the methods be used which I prescribe, & that your Lordship would pardon this freedome which is only zeale in.

Your Lps most obedient humble servant

Chr. Wren

By late June there is a new cause for concern. Wren has now received from the dean a plan of the existing structure that differs radi-

cally from an earlier plan on which he had based his design.

I thinke I have reckoned all particulars, according to my designes I sent, but I am confounded by the last peece of groundplot. I wrought by the first Groundplot which differe exceedingly from this. In the first I had 3 foot 9 inches between the inside of the inward Gate (measuring in the Torus's) & the inward angle; in this draught I have but 2 foot; in the first the College wall & the walls of the Gate are of one thicknesse 4 foot 3 inches. In this the sides of the porch are near 5 foot, & the College Wall not full 4 foot. If this be trew, I must correct many things in the Designe to adjust it as it should be, & I am uncertain whether I have the roome I desire for the peers that are to be added.

In the same letter, Wren instructs Bishop Fell on the methods of paying his stonemasons. He is careful to advise the dean to strike a good bargain but, at the same time, to make sure that the contractors are not held to unrealistically low estimates,

. . . for in things they are not every day used to, they doe often injure themselves, & when they are begin to find it, they shuffle and slight the worke to save themselves.

His recommendation:

I thinke the best way in this businesse is to worke by measure; according to the prices in the Estimate or lower if you can, & measure the work at 3 or 4 measurements as it rises. But you must have an understanding trusty Measurer, there are few that are skilled in measuring stone worke, I have bred up 2 or 3. Mr. Kempster will wait on you the beginning of the weeke. . . .

Uncertainties over the groundplot continue through the next letter (June 30), by which time Wren is requesting that his friend Kempster draw up a new one, ". . . soe from two witnesses wee shall find out the trewth." He asks the dean to halt all work until this is done. The confusion is causing delays, but Wren reminds

his impatient client:

I trouble your Lordship with scrupulosities but a thing well settled at first prevents more trouble, and errors in building are often incorrigible, & to peece well is a more carefull businesse than to erect a new thing where there is noe constraint, & that which is to last 500 yeares is not to be precipitated.

You may doe enough this yeare to finish the next, & sooner will not be safe.

Next Wren's "perfect estimate" needs to be revised upward. The fourth letter is undated but apparently belongs to the summer months following the first three. By this time Kempster is on the scene and is supervising the stonemasons, which Wren predicts "will be apt to mend their pace." But the costs? Well,

I have sent the articles, & because I find it hardly practible to drawe positive articles for every thing in such kind of worke as this is, but that there will be just reason to make small variations, & some things will be added to the worke as the hard stone,

19

& some larger Heddington stone then Ashler, (which was before omitted) and more is taken down than I suspected at first to be necessary, upon these considerations I have added such Clauses as will keepe us from quarrelling at last, & between honest men I thinke if handes be set to the Articles as they stand it may suffice. . . .

But the real problem is still to come. Since the bishop's letters did not survive along with Wren's, it's unclear how much of the cost revision was due to changes he insisted on, and it would be unlike the ever-tactful Wren to point the finger at his client unless the cost figures were challenged. The next change to be considered is clearly the bishop's idea, and it's a classic. Wren would need all of his tact and some very special expertise to deal with this one.

By December the work is progressing well, as Wren acknowledges in the first few lines of a letter dated December 3. He does not mention how much of the structure is erected, but his original schedule to Bishop Fell in May had been, ". . . You may begin presently & rayse the peeres & tracery vault then let it rest and settle, let mortars drie, & finish next summer."

The bishop, however, has had an inspiration. Sometime in early winter he has contacted Wren to propose that Tom Tower become not simply a bell tower over the gatehouse but, instead, *an astronomical observatory!* This, it occurs to him, might gain the college some leverage in getting contributions to finance the project.

If, in fact, his ninety-one years were free of profanity, this must have been one of Wren's closer calls. Suddenly his gate tower, begun "in the Gothick manner," had lost its point. Designed to rise to Gothic pinnacles and spire, it

Wren's tower gate to the quadrangle entrance has become a landmark at Oxford.

21

PLAN AA

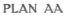

PLAN B·B   PLAN C C

would now have to be contorted into a flat-roof building to accommodate an observatory.

The architect had spent his whole early life as an astronomer, and he had just finished the building of Greenwich observatory. That structure (which is designed with a touch of the wizard's mystique, a sort of Merlin's castle) was envisioned, in Wren's words, ". . . for the Observators habitation & a little for pompe." The actual observations, he points out, are made not from the lofty platforms but from the court or the garden; the building is for apartments, offices, storage of instruments not in use, and, to suit His Majesty, "a little for pompe."

As for turning Tom Tower into an observatory, Wren seems at first to accept the notion and proceed to discuss what it will require to execute it.

Yet I doe not reject your Lordship's proposition of making it into an Observatory, & I was willing first to get rid of severall businesses that incombred me at once the last weeke that I might at leasure con-

sider of this change, for a change it will be of the whole designe.

As to Wren's "severall businesses," it should be noted that at this time he had the building of St. Paul's Cathedral well under way as well as his famed Trinity College Library, Kilmainham hospital, and at least a dozen London churches, rebuilding after the Great Fire. And as Surveyor of the King's Works, he was constantly on call for consultations regarding every piece of royal construction or remodeling. Still his attention to Bishop Fell was thorough, deferential—at least to a point—and devastating.

Detailing the necessary changes, he reports:

The loft for the Bell above the ringing loft must be higher considerable & with large Windowes & still I doubt the Bell will be somewhat lowe to be well heard; then the octagonall Tower must be flat on the top with a levell Ballaster (for pinnacles will doe injury) the windowes also must be only wooden shutters without Mullions for barres, these things

PLAN E·E

PLAN D·D

ARCH OVER

ARCH OVER

HATCHED PORTION SHOWS
WREN'S ADDITIONS TO OBTAIN
A SQUARE VAULT

Wren used his genius to calculate exact measurements to make sure that the tower was engineered properly. It was necessary to construct the tower so that it would be able to withstand vibrations when the huge bell rang.

considered it will necessarily fall short of the beauty of the other way, for having begun in the Gothick manner wee must conclude above with flats & such proportions as will not be well reconcilable to the Gothick which spires upward & the pyramidall formes are essentiall to it, & this proposition had been much better effected had not the parts formerly built diverted us from beginning after the better formes of Architecture, & I feare wee shall make an unhandsome medly this way.

Wren goes on to describe how astronomical observations are made and with what equipment, pointing out that there is nothing about a tower which contributes to this work, ". . . for wee valewe noe observations made near the Horizon." He concludes the letter by promising to start over with the whole design if the bishop persists in his plan, but then adds a postscript which surely must have destroyed the whole idea once and for all:

I cannot but adde thise Line that supposing all the

necessary instruments provided for an observatory (& I dare undertake for the Charge of 300 lb or 400 lb at most to provide more usefull and accurate instruments than I find were ever yet made) *I will then for lesse charge than a pidgeon house provide all the housing necessary.*

Nine months later, Tom Tower stood complete, as originally designed, awaiting only a ball and vane for the top of the spire and the hanging of Great Tom itself. The custom soon developed that when the big bell began to toll at nine each evening, students of the college knew they had exactly 101 bongs to get back into the quadrangle before the gates clanged shut for the night. No one knows what those mighty vibrations might have done to the calibrations of astronomical instruments, but nearly three hundred years of wear and tear haven't opened a single "unexcusable" flaw or crack in Tom Tower, whose hard stones were, after some difficulty, "well peeced and set in the trew waies."

IRELAND'S CURIOUS TOWERS

After a thousand years
no one could remember
how they got there

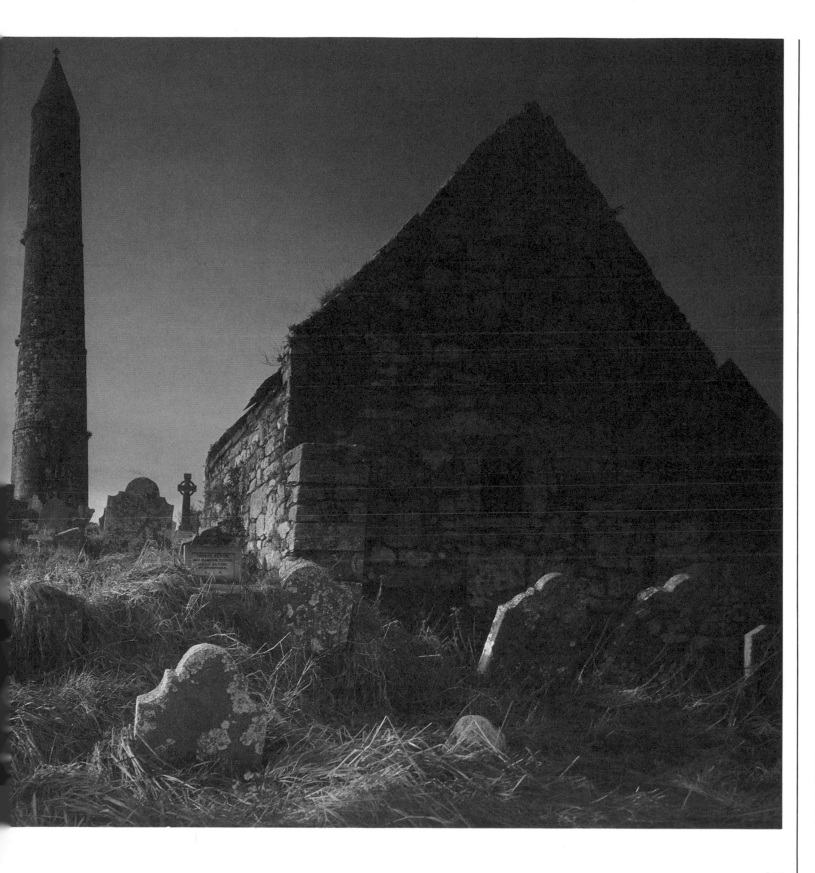

At Ardmore in County Waterford, amid tombstones and crosses dating from the same remote period, stands one of Ireland's Round Towers, an odd but wonderfully durable tribute to Irish resourcefulness.

Picture a medieval Irish monk . . . at a dead run. And sixty more or seventy: a monastery in turmoil, triggered by the tinkling of one small hand bell from the top of a tower. Utensils clatter to the floor in the scullery and the dining hall where the community has just finished breakfast. Someone is hurriedly stoking a tinderbox; others gather what they can carry of food staples and water. In the church sacristy, monks are hastily collecting prayer books, religious relics, and the sacred vessels. And out of the drafty hard bench halls, where reading, teaching, and the copying of documents had just begun for the day, students and their cleric teachers are running, their arms laden with irreplaceable texts and manuscripts. Here at Ardmore in County Waterford, as elsewhere in twelfth-century Ireland, virtually every scrap of written knowledge and tradition exists solely because the men of the monasteries have painstakingly recorded and preserved it.

But now they must save not only the manuscripts but themselves. The bell ringing is increasingly frantic. Some of the monks have reached the tower from which the warning signal sounded—a curious, pencil-shaped stone spire rising 130 feet to its conical belfry. From nearby farms people who have head the commotion or sighted its cause are arriving, breathless and frightened, to join the monks. One by one they scramble up a ladder to the single entry—ten feet off the ground. Finally, everyone is inside, the ladder is pulled in after them, and the heavy wooden door slams shut.

In the midnineteenth century, Irish scholar George Petrie made the first systematic survey of his country's ancient towers. It was Petrie who pointed out that the Round Towers were invariably found among monastic ruins.

From the far side of the monastery, toward the bay, an awesome sight has emerged: the dreaded horned helmets, boar skins, heavy swords, shields, and bloodcurdling shouts in the unrecognizable tongue of the Norse invaders, landed in one of their countless raids on the villages and monasteries of England and Ireland. As a tribute to Odin, and to the ship's stores, they will sack the monastery. They will burn every book and parchment abandoned in panic. They will carry off whatever treasures have been unsuccessfully hidden. And, if they have the time and patience, they will outwait and possibly try to root out or burn out the refugees in the tower. But that will be a job.

The Round Towers of Ireland were so sturdy that eighty of them are still standing today, even where the churches and abbeys around them lie in rubble or have been leveled and overgrown for nearly a thousand years. The Towers did not succeed in saving Irish scholarship or in safeguarding any substantial percentage of the art and literature that flourished there despite the encircling Dark Ages. But they did save whatever *was* saved, and sometimes they saved the people who lived in constant peril from the Viking raiders, who came and went at will for several hundred years.

Woefully cramped for a refuge in siege, the Towers were nevertheless hard to breach. No warriors defended the portals—the occupants were conspicuously nonmilitary—but the single door was heavy, heavily bolted, and elevated beyond the reach of battering rams. The stone walls were at least three, sometimes five feet thick at the base. Windows were small, only one window per story, each facing in a different direction. Inside, there were from three to five floors, each a separate compartment connected to the one below only by a ladder, which could be retracted to the room above, and the opening sealed to keep out attackers

Ranging from four to eight stories, the Round Towers stand 60 to 130 feet high and 40 to 60 feet in circumference. Floor levels are often visible from the outside as stone bands or holes in the walls.

29

Grave markers, grottoes, and Irish high crosses are usually among the ruins around Round Tower sites. When some of the original church and monastery stonework is still intact, it shows masonry methods very similar to that of the surviving towers.

or smoke. Eventually, the invaders might burn out their prisoners, or starve them out, but the task was so lengthy and so difficult—while the main booty was in the monastery, not the tower—that the brothers very often survived the raids.

As for the towers, they often survived not only one raid but many, endured through 300 years of predatory Norsemen, finally outlasted the churches and monasteries they were built to serve, then stood for nearly a thousand years of disuse while the surrounding inhabitants entirely forgot how these curious structures ever rose to punctuate the Irish landscape.

When someone finally asked how the Round Towers came to be, the flowering of theories was remarkable. The Druids built them, one antiquary announced, as places from which to proclaim religious festivals. No, it was the Danes, or the Carthaginians, or the Phoenicians. The sloping window jambs of several towers led someone to connect them with the temples of ancient Egypt. Perhaps they were fire temples, possibly astronomical observatories, prisons, Buddhist temples, monastic castles, temples of Baal, beacons, watchtowers, stylite columns, or phallic emblems.

In 1845 Irish scholar George Petrie drove the

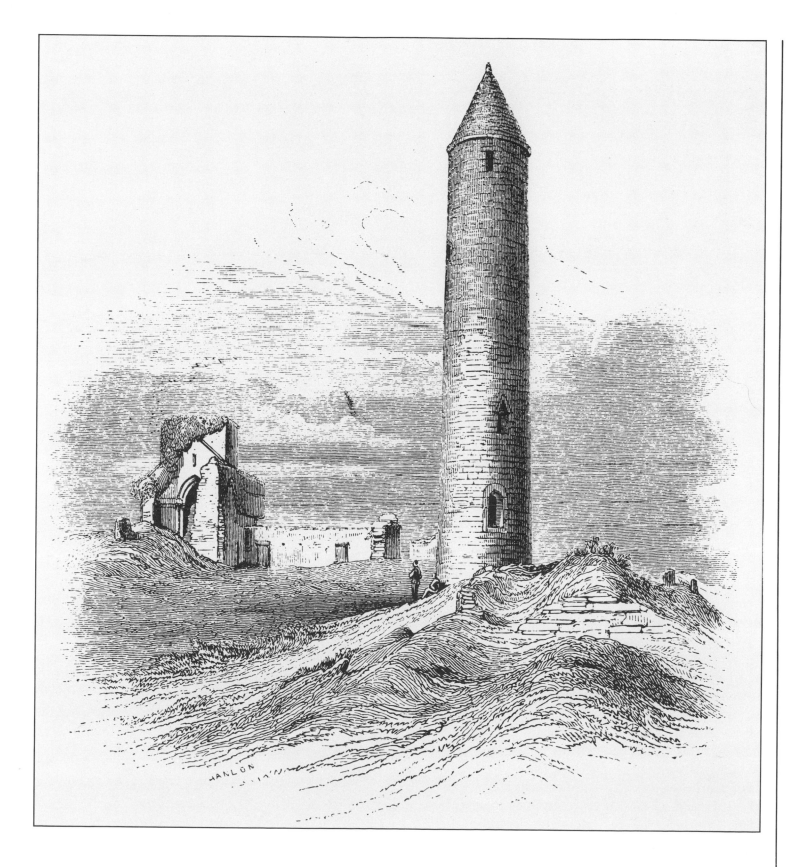

As many as twenty Viking raids on a single monastery were recorded between the years 800 and 1100. Monks took refuge in their towers to save themselves and whatever they could carry of the art and literature that would otherwise have perished during Europe's Dark Ages.

31

Many of the towers withstood 300 years of Viking incursions and have outlasted their mother monasteries by nearly a thousand years more. Kilree Tower still stands, almost completely intact, among ruins of the ecclesiastical buildings it once served.

bats out of the belfry with a careful, methodical analysis, establishing once and for all that the towers were Christian in origin (in fact, had Christian emblems in some cases), that they were always built in conjunction with monasteries, that their architectural features were unrelated to any remnant of pre-Christian structures in Ireland but closely related to their companion church buildings, that all were built during the period of Viking colonization and plunder, and that their uses included both the function of bell tower and that of refuge for "passive defence" in time of siege.

To that Margaret Stokes added the clincher in her 1878 volume, *Early Christian Architecture in Ireland*. She chronicled the Norse raiding patterns that inflicted up to twenty recorded raids on a single monastery between 800 and 1100. Then, having shown the need for a secure refuge to preserve men and property, she returned to the architectural evidence and made a shrewd series of observations about tower windows.

Although each window commands a different side, there is almost always one window directly above the door. And while the other

Virtually every Round Tower has a window directly over the door, its sill sloping outward. Anyone trying to force entry through the door would have to stand in bull's-eye position for anything the defenders decided to drop or pour through the window.

windows may be placed high on the walls of their respective rooms for maximum light, the window over the door is close to the floor, and its sill slopes downward to the outside.

How that configuration would suit a Druid festival or the worship of Baal was hard to imagine—but it would certainly accommodate the dropping of heavy things on an attacker who was trying to breach the tower's only door.

Once this sort of systematic study had begun, other patterns emerged. All told, there were some 120 towers in Ireland, others in Scotland. Of the seventy-five or eighty survivors, twenty are almost totally intact. They range from 60 to 130 feet in height, from 40 to 60 feet in circumference, or only 13 to 19 feet in diameter. Each has from four to eight stories, roughly twelve feet in height. Demarcation between floors is often visible from the outside, either in the form of stone bands or of holes left in the walls to receive joists. Floors were usually wood, though a few were of stone, slightly arched.

The first towers were built of rubble masonry. Small stones, shaped by hammer, were fitted into the interstices between larger stones, all secured by lime mortar—a technique shared

33

Christian emblems, mingled with secular embellishments of the day, began to appear in and around later examples of Round Tower design— arches, corbels, and carvings adding grace notes to the pure survival features of earlier towers.

by many of the early Irish churches. Later examples, such as the Ardmore tower pictured here, show progress in masonry to fine ashlar work, along with a limited evolution in architectural nuance. Lintels, triangular arches, and primitive entablature for doors and windows gradually gave way to Romanesque arches as Irish missionaries returned from the European continent. Also, a modicum of decorative work began to appear: corbels and carvings around windows and doors and in the belfries.

But compared with the intricate scriptural scenes and signs of the Irish High Crosses dating from the same period—in fact often sharing the same sites—the Round Towers remained plainly functional. Their roundness, their solid masonry bases, thick walls, slight taper, and

double doors with heavy iron fittings all contributed to their amazing permanence through a period when virtually everything else was laid to waste.

Some were badly built. The tower of Kilmacduagh in County Galway leans 17 1/2 feet out of perpendicular, which is four feet further askew than the Tower of Pisa. Others simply fell down. But for a species born in a backward age of architecture—when what structural technology that did exist was oriented toward wood rather than stone—the Round Towers stand tall, each planted at the edge of an abbey graveyard but pointing in the direction singled out by the Irish monastic community as its purpose and destination.

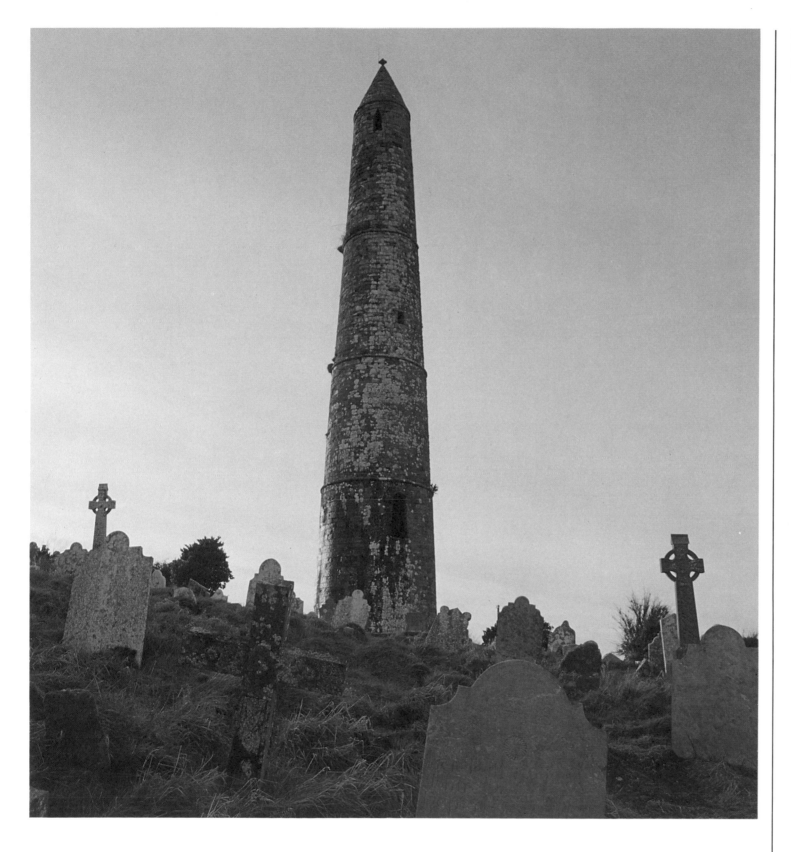

Fine ashlar stonework distinguishes the Ardmore tower as one of the later examples of Round Tower design.

E-TEMEN-ANKI

The Tower of Babel

"Come, let us make a city and a tower, the top whereof may reach to heaven. . . ."

Genesis xi:4

The Egyptians dug straight down and introduced the well. The Phoenicians headed out to sea and broadened the ancient world's idea of commerce. For the Sumerians the direction was up, and the result was the Tower of Babel.

The facts are buried forty centuries deep in history and lore. Just as no one is sure how deep the Egyptians dug, or how far the Phoenicians roamed, historians are uncertain as to how high the Sumerians were able to build. Still, the outlines of the story and the rough outlines of the tower have been pieced together.

The theme of man as an overreacher—daring too much, challenging the gods, tampering with nature—has proved to be a persistent specter and one capable of many forms: Prometheus, Icarus, Faust, Manfred, Dr. Frankenstein, the Forbidden Fruit, the Panama Canal, and the nuclear bomb. Among artists, a favorite for centuries has been the biblical Tower of Babel, the human attempt to ascend into heaven without invitation. Several examples follow. Here, Brueghel's allegorical painting links the sins of the past and present by placing his tower near a busy Flemish seaport.

37

Courtesy of the British Museum

Roughly 4,000 years ago the Sumerians migrated from an arid Iranian plateau to the vast, fertile plain of Shinar in Mesopotamia. Here, on the banks of the Euphrates and Tigris rivers, they began to farm, to quarry, and to build.

Aided by history's first standardized system of measurement—and spurred by the Sumerian belief that gods should be lodged far above the common mortal—they soon punctuated the plain with towering temples called ziggurats, jutting high above the flat city roofs to dominate a pilgrim's view from miles away.

By far the most conspicuous of the ziggurats stood in the city of Ka-dingir ("Gate of God"). When the city was conquered by the Semites, the name was literally translated to Bab-ilu. The tower was called E-temen-anki ("House of the Foundation of Heaven and Earth"). Translators of the Old Testament baptized the temple "The Tower of Babel."

The Bible recounts how "brick for stone, and bitumen for mortar" were used to raise the tower heavenward, only to have the builders struck with "confusion of tongues" for their presumption.[1]

Whatever "confusion of tongues" may mean, there is at this point a confusion of legend. The most durable version of this story cast Babel in a role similar to Eve's apple: after challenging heaven with a tower, man was driven out of his linguistic Garden of Eden—where everyone spoke the same language—and was doomed to a world of many nations speaking many languages.

This, however, is not necessarily the biblical version; Genesis acknowledges the existence of different languages in the chapter preceding the account of Babel. Nor is it the archaeological version. Scholars have established that at least two languages—Sumerian and Semitic—

1. A conflicting Mesopotamian legend tells how Nimrod, the Hunter (Gen. x:9) instigated a rebellion against the god who annihilated the world with a flood. Nimrod persuaded the rebels to build a tower high enough to escape the ravaging waters in case of another deluge.

Mosaic from San Marco, Venice; photo, Scala, New York/Venice

According to Genesis, the people of Babylon said, "Come, let us build ourselves a city, and a tower with its top in the heavens, and let us make a name for ourselves." The Lord descended on their presumption by "confusing their tongues," making them unable to understand each other, thus unable to finish the tower.

In Macedonian legend the tower was built by Nimrod, the Hunter, who instructed his followers to raise a tower tall enough to escape from any future floods imposed by heaven.

coexisted in Babylon prior to the tower.

It's possible that the entire "confusion of tongues" legend is traceable to a translator's error. The Akkadian word *bab-ilu* ("gate of God") is close to the Hebrew verb *balal* ("to confuse").

Whatever the case, the Tower of Babel *did* exist early in Babylonian history. Cuneiform texts, carved reliefs on ancient trays and urns, and detailed studies of the chronology of the Old Testament all attest that the great ziggurat was first raised as early as the Sumerians or their immediate conquerors.

But, as the war-torn Babylonian Dynasty faltered and eventually perished, the tower's sundried bricks fell prey to time and conquerors. (Some archaeologists contend that it was in ruins during Hammurabi's reign, around 1790 B.C.) And it was not until the reign of Nabopolassar (626-605 B.C.) that Babylon and its historic tower returned to glory.

Nabopolassar and Nebuchadnezzar, his son

The Bettmann Archive, Inc.

Once destroyed, the Tower of Babel was rebuilt by Nebuchadnezzar as part of a grander scheme to restore Babylon as the most spectacular city in the world.

and successor, rebuilt Babylon on a spectacular scale. The city was crammed with wonders of the world: the celebrated Hanging Gardens . . . the garish Ishtar Gate with enameled-brick reliefs of bulls and dragons . . . brilliantly colored, 23-foot-thick walls that lined the procession path to the sacred zone of Marduk, the Lord of Eternal Life . . . and, most prominent, the detailed reconstruction of the original Tower of Babel. Once again, Babylon was the Capital City of the World.

Rebuilding the great ziggurat was the most ambitious task of all. His predecessors had made the mistake of using materials that quickly eroded; Nebuchadnezzar employed harder, properly fired bricks. Near the core of the eight-staged tower, the bricks were nearly forty-nine feet thick. According to one estimate, fifty-eight million bricks went into E-temen-anki.

The tower stood in a thick-walled, 500-yard by 450-yard enclosure, surrounded by small basilica-like chapels, pilgrim cottages, and a

Courtesy of The Pierpont Morgan Library

smaller temple called E-sagila, which housed a pure gold statue of the god Marduk. Herodotus, the Greek Historian, who visited Babylon, estimated the weight of the statue and other gold objects in the small temple at 800 talents. Estimated worth today: $85,000,000.

Information garnered from an excavated tablet shows that the Tower of Babel had a square foundation, each side measuring slightly over 298 feet. Like an immense wedding cake, it rose in eight superimposed stages, each story smaller than the preceding one, to a height of 300 feet. Gigantic lateral stairways extended approximately one hundred feet up the tower to the first story, while another stairway, situated perpendicular to the face of the wall, led to the second story. From these points ascent was made by means of a series of secret ramps and stairwells to the top. Couches for resting were positioned at various spots along the climb.

At the summit of E-temen-anki, Marduk resided in a small temple, or *shahuru*. The walls of this temple were gold-plated and decorated with bright blue enameled bricks. The room was empty but for a richly adorned couch (for Marduk to rest) and a gilded table. The only human permitted to enter this sanctuary was a woman, chosen by Marduk's priests to give the god "pleasure."

Imagine the sight that the multitudes of pil-

The Bettmann Archive, Inc.

grims beheld when they came to Babylon for the annual two-day procession for the god Marduk. As they entered the enclosure through Babu-Ellu ("Holy Gate"), they would worship the pure gold statue in E-sagila, go up the stairway and scan the entire city, craning their necks to see the desert sun on the blue and gold walls of the *shahuru.*

However, the glory of the Tower of Babel did not last long. It did survive the city's capture by Cyrus the Persian (539 B.C.), who became so fascinated by the colossality of the structure that he ordered a smaller E-temen-anki be built for his grave; but the tower fell when Xerxes leveled Babylon nearly a century later.

Alexander the Great, leading his army through Babylonia on an expedition to India, ordered 10,000 of his soldiers to clear away the debris from the tower. He had to forsake the task eventually, but only after his army had spent a total of 600,000 workdays on the project.

Soon local inhabitants began carting away the hard building material for their own purposes, reminiscent of how the Vatican was built from the debris of Roman temples. Even today, a dam that diverts the Euphrates river into a canal is made of bricks that bear Nebuchadnezzar's royal stamp, while the site of the most famous religious tower in antiquity is nothing but a watery hole in the ground.

When the architects are ghosts
the house is of course a nightmare

DESIGNS FOR THE HAUNTED HOUSE

It ought to be possible to design a house in such a way that its occupants never see a ghost. The techniques for baffling, frightening, and denying access to would-be haunts are neither precise nor entirely consistent, but they are abundant.

What is vastly more difficult, judging from the ghostly lore, is the deliberate effort to design a haunted house—to achieve the character, the ambience, and the specific features that will invite ghosts to appear. It has been seriously attempted at least once, and that attempt took thirty-six years of construction and an investment of at least $5 million.

Winchester House photographs by Ed Zak

The Winchester House—designed in every particular to attract friendly ghosts and repel hostile ones. Based on plans received each evening in séance, a nine-room house added over 700 more rooms in 38 years of unceasing construction, consuming a substantial fraction of the Winchester Rifle fortune.

The bell tower remained silent until midnight. Neighbors found it hard to explain (but the ghosts knew) why the only hours tolled were midnight, one and two.

Money was no problem for Sarah Pardee Winchester. As a young woman, she inherited all the wealth generated by the invention and manufacture of the Winchester repeating rifle. Her problem, as she saw it and as an eager Boston spiritualist quickly verified, was the likelihood of vengeful ghosts.

The rifle had dispatched thousands of unwilling souls into the spirit world, all prematurely, none happily. If they came back, they would come back in unpleasant moods, and they would include in their number some very unpleasant types: frontier rowdies, murderers, bandits, drunks, and—most terrifying of all in Mrs. Winchester's mind—Indians!

With an ample construction budget and a retinue of willing spiritualists to advise her, Mrs. Winchester could have commissioned the design of a virtually foolproof, ghostproof house.

For example, although it is not clear why ghosts hate mirrors, it seems very clear to ghost watchers that they do. Confronted by a mirror, the apparitions vanish—some say because they are terrified by their own reflections; others say because ghosts are embarrassed or offended by the fact they have no reflections.

A house built with mirror walls in all rooms should be entirely free of hauntings. Short of that, a house designed without chimneys would deprive many ghosts of their favorite access and avenue of escape. A house surrounded by a moat is safe from the large majority of ghosts who can't or won't cross water. Towers and balconies should be eliminated; and since ghosts worry about time but depend on earthly timepieces (they normally arrive at or after midnight and must depart by two), clocks are taboo and bell towers are out of the question.

But to Mrs. Winchester the problem was not so simple. Her fear was not only that vindictive ghosts would haunt her while she lived but also that they would ostracize her in the here-

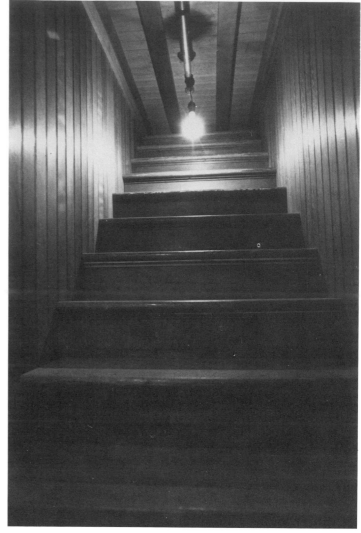

after. At the same time she had been assured that there were good ghosts as well as bad ones, and that the better spirits, properly appeased, would protect her in life and welcome her into polite society after death.

Through one of the spiritualists she also received word that no harm would come to her as long as builders were busy providing accommodations for the friendly spirits who would keep unfriendly spirits away.

So Mrs. Winchester began to build her house. From Boston she moved to California in 1884 and there bought a nine-room ranch

house near San Jose. She hired twenty carpenters, soon added masons, glaziers, plumbers, and eventually electricians, and seven Japanese gardeners whose task was to raise and maintain a high hedge that would wrap the place in total privacy. Shifts were arranged so that the sound of hammers would continue year-round and around the clock.

Design conferences took place in the Séance Room, where Mrs. Winchester sat each evening, apparently alone. Her ghostly consultants were numerous but untrained, capricious, often vague, and utterly insatiable—demanding

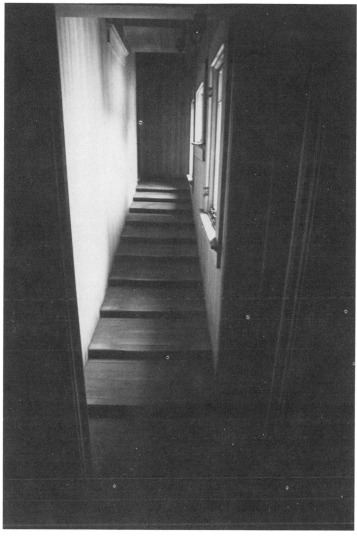

After the widow's death, it took six weeks just to remove the furniture. Movers frequently found themselves trapped behind one-way doors, lost in labyrinthine corridors, and frustrated by endless, aimless staircases. Seven stories tall at its highest point, the house boasted more stairs than the Tower of Babel.

room after room, balcony after balcony, chimney after chimney. No mirrors. No moat. Forty-seven fireplaces, dozens of clocks (including three of the costliest chronometers in existence), watchtowers, a bell tower, and such personalized features as a floor made of seven kinds of hardwood and a stairway with seven turns and forty-four risers to ascend only nine feet.

The place was being designed by ghosts and for ghosts. Each morning plans drawn the previous night were handed to the head carpenter by Mrs. Winchester's personal secretary. No one else was permitted to see the widow. (Teddy

Roosevelt once paid a call and was refused an audience. When she moved around the house, Mrs. Winchester wore a veil, and when two workmen accidentally saw her without it, they were discharged with a year's pay.)

At first these makeshift blueprints were nearly indecipherable and often unbuildable. As time went on, however, the drawings improved—even if their logic did not. To nine rooms were added dozens more, and finally hundreds more, many of them soon ripped out to make way for new ideas from Mrs. Winchester's nocturnal advisors. From its original site

Bizarre in its sprawling caricature of Victorian architecture, the Winchester House is exquisite nonetheless in some of its detail. Every balcony, turret, and cornice received lavish attention to craftsmanship, and original stained and art glass designs decorate windows and doors. Glass for the front door alone cost $2,000.

The sun porch (top right) has a "skylight" in the floor, revealing nothing but a blank ceiling above and a hardwood floor below. One window pane in the room is made of optical glass serving as a lens to magnify the scenery—or possibly to prevent mirrored flat-glass reflections that might offend a benevolent ghost.

There are no master blueprints of the Winchester House. It was built and rebuilt from séance to séance, new plans materializing each morning. Instructions for the carpenters, masons, and glaziers were sketched by Mrs. Winchester on separate scraps of paper or the séance room tablecloth.

the house soon spread, crawling across a meadow to surround and swallow a nearby barn. A watchtower would rise, only to be engulfed by new layers of additions until its entire view was blocked.

Today, 160 rooms of this baffling labyrinth still stand, the survivors of an estimated 750 chambers, interconnected—if that is the word—by dead-end stairways, trick doors, self-intersecting balconies, and one stairway that goes down to a landing from which there is no other course except another stairway going up.

When Mrs. Winchester died in 1922, it took six weeks just to remove the furniture, partly because movers were continually going through one-way doors, finding themselves trapped and then lost for hours on end as they followed stairs to blank walls and corridors to unopenable doors.

Of her $21-million inheritance the widow had spent at least $5 million to please her discorporate friends. Unless ghosts are unspeakable ingrates, Mrs. Winchester has been well received and well regarded ever since.

If the building of the Winchester House seems eccentric to persons who do not take ghosts seriously, it must seem even more bizarre to those who do—or to the ghosts themselves.

In the thousands of recorded ghost appearances and the probable millions of unpublicized reports, the one reliable common denominator is that ghosts of the departed are seen and heard where the departed actually departed.

A Plains Indian might return to ride where he once rode, to hunt in the hills where he once hunted, to reenact the murder or the battle that did him in. But travel to California? Track down the whole chain of cause and effect from bullet to rifle to factory to owner to heir, and then leave his favorite haunts for a strange town? It would be most unghostlike.

By the established norms of haunting, all

Baffling doors enabled Mrs. Winchester to elude evil spirits, especially the big, mean ones. Small in stature, she could enter the regular door on the left, then duck back through the small one, leaving the ghost to bang his head. Other doors are concealed, disguised, or armed with one-way latches to permit entry but no exit.

Mrs. Winchester had to do was determine that the original nine-room house she was buying (a) had not been haunted before, and (b) did not belong to General Custer.

What happened in that Séance Room night after night is a secret buried with the widow, but if she was convinced that her ghosts were passionately particular about design details for the building, then she was dealing with a most unusual species of spook.

It's true that there are creaking old manor houses which appear perfect for haunting. There are castles in England, Scandinavia, France, Germany, Italy, and Spain where ghosts are nothing short of mandatory, especially when the time comes to attract tourists.

People respond—albeit some people more than others—to a sense of strangeness, of mystery, most often in dark, damp, drafty, and preferably very old dwellings. And certain architectural features seem to heighten this susceptibility to haunting: windowless attics, long corridors, cavernous basements, steep gables, belfries, balconies, towers, widow's walks, dramatic staircases, lone and lofty windows, and deep, bat-sheltering eaves.

But the ghosts themselves show a profound indifference to any such distinctions. Their choices of places to appear are almost without discrimination as to architecture. They are reported not only in deep-dungeoned castles and ornate Victorian mansions but just as often

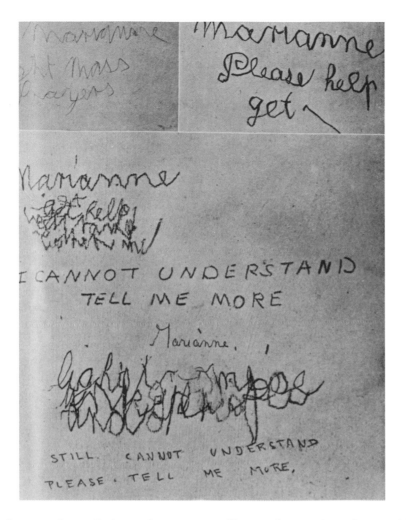

Built in 1865 about sixty miles from London, Borley Rectory has been called "the most haunted house in England." Repeated sightings of a ghostly nun, sometimes by three and four witnesses together, were followed by the report of a horse-drawn coach that appeared and then vanished, mysterious sounds of hoofbeats and of a dog howling, then by so-called poltergeist phenomena: the falling and breaking of various household objects for no apparent cause.

When a team of investigators rented the rectory in 1937 (it had become too spooky to hold a normal tenant), the nun reappeared several times, poltergeist manifestations continued, and odd messages appeared on the walls (left), sometimes forming under the eyes of the researchers. When the rectory burned in 1939, the investigators had it excavated. A woman's skeleton was found under the cellar floor.

in simple farmhouses, barns, box-Colonial subdivisions, and apartments—even in a cinderblock army post building in Texas and a topless nightclub in Toronto. The one possible exception is that it is very hard to find stories of haunted high-rise office buildings.

What matters to the ghost, in the great preponderance of reported cases, is what happened to him, not where or in what surroundings. A child who has witnessed a grisly murder returns to the scene. A man hanged by mistake lingers to clear his name. In most accounts of hauntings that claim to be true, the spirit comes back to erase, reenact, avenge, or simply continue to brood about some awful event or unfulfilled longing.

If so, the only ghosts likely to care a great deal about architecture would be the ghosts of architects. The notions that people have of what a haunted house is supposed to look like seem to spring from the fears of the living, their responses to unfamiliar surroundings, and from design decisions made not by architects or by ghosts but by writers: Edgar Allen Poe and kindred spirits fueling two hundred years of public enchantment with mysterious tales and the so-called Gothic novel. These and latter-day tendencies, such as the merchandising of Halloween, seem to have frozen a haunted house sterotype that the haunts themselves do not recognize.

"Oh! The Purple Abbots! What a spot they had chosen to slumber in!" So sang Horace Walpole of the ruins of Netley Abbey (top, center). The abbots may have been purple in the thirteenth century when Netley flourished, but the one who returned 400 years later was completely white.

One of the lesser centers of medieval scholarship and religious life, Netley stood across Southhampton Water from a much larger monastery, Beaulieu, which is now completely gone, its stones long since shipped down the Exe for the building of Hearst Castle. Both monasteries were closed and partially destroyed by Henry VIII in his reform of the church.

In 1700, one Walter Taylor bought the abbey church at Netley to sell its stone but declined to supervise the dismantling. He had been visited by the whitened ghost of an old Cistercian monk who warned him that if he moved these sacred stones, the roof would fall on him. Taylor had the entire roof and central tower removed before he would set foot inside. When he did, the tracery of the main west window fell off and fractured his skull.

Not far from the haunts of Rip Van Winkle and Ichabod Crane, the U.S. Military Academy at West Point has had its share of Hudson ghosts. The shade of a nineteenth-century maid named Molly is said to rumple the bedclothes in the superintendent's mansion (top, left). A woman who died in a nearby house frightens guests by floating in through an upstairs window. And recently, two cadets in the 47th Division barracks reported several visits by a nineteenth-century cavalry officer in full regalia.

Though not famed for its own haunts, Strawberry Hill (bottom, left) is in some sense first in the architectural line of the haunted house. It was the home of Horace Walpole, author of the prototype supernatural novel, *The Castle of Otranto*. Strawberry Hill was built as a sham ruin in the spirit of the Gothic revival that Walpole helped to lead. Unable to finance the full replication of a Gothic castle, he had pasteboard battlements added to his turrets and, inside, fake flutings and groinings painted on where he couldn't afford to have them carved.

The William Lyon Mackenzie Homestead in Toronto (top, right) was once occupied by Toronto's first mayor (grandfather of Canada's later statesman, Mackenzie King). It is now a national shrine—and a celebrated haunted house where ghosts have repeatedly been seen and have been heard tramping the steps and pounding the piano. One has been described as the original Mackenzie; dead over a hundred years. Another, a woman, has been sighted by employees and reporters, and she once slapped a resident housekeeper.

Emily Bronte's *Wuthering Heights* (bottom, right) might best be described as a haunting romance. After loving and losing, Heathcliff and Cathy in turn haunt the storm-swept fictional manor house—first Cathy, whose ghost tries to enter an upstairs window; and later Heathcliff, who is said to walk the halls and grounds after his death.

Ford's Theater in Washington (top, right), where Lincoln was shot, has had recurrent reports of the ghost of John Wilkes Booth. Bootsteps are heard, portraits tilt, actors get strange chills, and a Matthew Brady photograph of the empty theater the day after Lincoln's assassination shows an eerie, disproportionate transparent figure close to the president's box.

(Top, center) Fontill Abbey. Like Walpole, William Beckford was swept up in the Gothic revival and its obsession with the picturesque. In 1796, he asked James Wyatt to design him a ruined convent of which only part had survived. He prodded the builders to work around the clock, changed the design until it was no longer Gothic, lived proudly in it for a few years, then sold it. Haste had bred oversights: the foundation stones for the central tower, for example, had been omitted. In 1825, sham ruins became real ruins when the tower sank into the rest.

Nathaniel Hawthorne's *House of Seven Gables* (top, left) stands under the curse of a wizard who was executed during the Salem witch trials. It comes complete with a secret compartment behind the portrait of Colonel Pyncheon, its original owner, and three generations of Pyncheon men who died in the oak chair under the portrait.

(Bottom, left) A haunted house in Washington, D.C.

With its 800-year history of murders and executions, the Tower of London (bottom, center and right) has more cause for haunting than most places. Among other reported apparitions, visits by two executed wives of Henry VIII have gained the most notoriety. Katherine Howard has appeared many times. In 1864, an iridescent Anne Boleyn approached a guard, who first tried to bayonet her, then fainted and was court-martialed for sleeping on duty. He was acquitted when the commander of the guard reluctantly admitted that he had been at an upstairs window and had seen the entire incident, ghost and all.

MACHU PICCHU

Lost city of the Incas

The role of scapegoat in history, before it was preempted by politicians, was occupied largely by architects and writers. When war, disaster, or disease left a culture wondering whom to blame, the usual response was to raze the architect's monuments and temples and burn the writer's chronicles. And when invaders judged a conquered people to be wrongheaded or lazy, the army straightaway destroyed the books and buildings around which the offending culture was patterned.

Tucked away high in the Andes, its location a secret and its existence a mere rumor, Machu Picchu escaped Pizarro's devastating conquest of Peru and remained an unconfirmed legend until early in this century.
George Holton from Photo Researchers

Had they found this fabled city, the Spanish conquistadors would have been disappointed. The streets were not, after all, paved with gold. But for the Yale expedition which eventually discovered Machu Picchu four hundred years later, here was the greatest archaeological treasure of all.

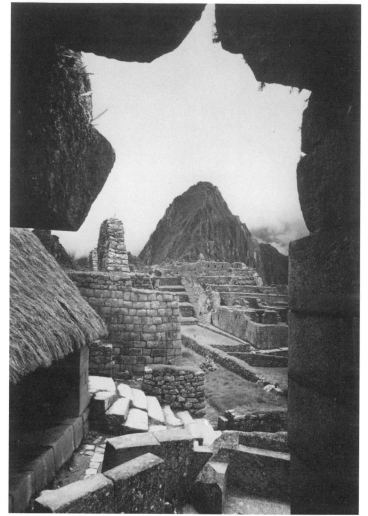

Michael Hayman from Photo Researchers

Legend has it that the Incas once possessed a written language but, regarding it as the cause of a great pestilence, banned its use under pain of death and forbade even the traffic in *quilcas*—the parchment or leaves used for writing. This one was on the writers; the next one was on the architects: Pizarro's conquistadors, confronted by a recalcitrant non-Christian population, destroyed its temples and leveled its cities.

For hundreds of years, the known remnants amounted to scattered fragments of a once-magnificent architecture and a few, highly suspect written accounts.

Historians nourished themselves mainly on W. H. Prescott's famous chronicles, which were based on the royal commentaries of Garcilaso de la Vega, the son of an Inca princess and a Spanish conquistador. But Garcilaso was making the most of dim memories. He had left Peru as a teenager and did not begin to reminisce until he was an old man in Spain.

Another account, compiled by Fernando Montesinos, was somewhat clouded by the author's belief that Peru was originally developed under Ophir, the great-grandson of Noah. And, lacking a written language, the Incas themselves were unable to set the record

Emil Schulthess from Black Star

Mortarless stone houses on the terraced slopes (below) attest to the ingenuity of Inca builders. No less ingenious as farmers and breeders, they developed the potato and the sweet potato from wild plants, and they domesticated llamas (left), which still graze around the fifteenth-century stonework long after the Incas have gone.

straight with any obliging equivalent of the Rosetta Stone or the Dead Sea Scrolls.

Into this vast historiographic vacuum trekked Hiram Bingham, in 1911, with a Yale expedition mounted to track down the persistent legend of a "Lost City of the Incas." Bingham's party sifted through rumors, pored over ancient maps, and began a ghastly trek down the Urubamba river, a headwater of the Amazon. Camped beneath a towering mountain called Machu Picchu, they heard that there were "interesting ruins" above. By this time the rigors of jungle travel had dampened some of the group's exploring zeal. The expedition naturalist could see no reason to climb a mountain when he could, at leisure, find more interesting specimens near the river. The surgeon wanted to wash his clothes. Bingham finally went up with a Peruvian army sergeant and found what is generally regarded as the most important archaeological discovery in the Western Hemisphere.

Here were a hundred, ten-foot-high stone-faced terraces—each hundreds of feet long. Here was a cave lined with beautifully cut stone—apparently a mausoleum for royalty. Here was a great curving wall made from fine-grain ashlars of pure-white granite—more

The American Museum of Natural History

61

With nothing more than stone implements, the Incas were able to build interlocking walls of perfectly carved and fitted stones. These stand, sturdy as ever, after hundreds of years in an area where earthquakes have often reduced more modern structures to rubble.

George Holton from Photo Researchers

The American Museum of Natural History

magnificent than any of the Cuzco walls which had been admired for centuries. Here was a flight of steps hewn from a single giant block of granite.

Here were houses with architectural details unique in all the world: stone pegs carved into the gable ends to secure roof thatching, eye-bonder courses drilled with sand and water to secure the roof purlins, massive bar locks carved from ten-ton doorway posts to secure the buildings against intruders. Here, without question, was the Lost City of the Incas.

In the view of its sixteenth-century inhabitants—and of today's scholars—Machu Picchu was fortunate to be "lost." Pizarro's conquistadors found Cuzco, the largest and most resplendent city of pre-Columbian America, and demolished it. They found Inca cities, Inca temples, and a luminous Inca culture throughout vast stretches of present-day Peru, Ecuador, Bolivia, Argentina, and Chile—and reduced it all to an impoverished serfdom. But in forty years of searching, they could not find Machu Picchu; so this remarkable monument to Inca genius survived the coming of "civilization."

Once Bingham had succeeded where Pizarro had failed, the evidence of Machu Picchu combined with other Inca ruins to reveal a startling record of architectural and engineering accomplishments. Examples:

The Incas were great irrigators. Without surveying instruments, they ran perfect contour lines dozens of miles through the valleys, and down from some of the highest, most rugged

By domesticating alpacas and llamas—both mountain relatives of the camel—the Incas probably saved these animals from extinction. Smaller than the llama, the alpaca was bred by the Incas for its fine wool.

mountains in the world. Aqueducts supplied the cities.

The Incas were prodigious wall builders. Near Cuzco there is a fort whose walls contain 300-ton blocks so perfectly mated that the cracks between them will not admit a knife blade. Without mortar, without clamps, without iron or steel tools, the Incas shaped these huge pieces by hammering them with rocks and honed smaller blocks with abrasive sand mixtures.

The Incas were great temple builders. When Pizarro's men invaded Cuzco, they tore down the mammoth Temple of the Sun and erected a church on its foundation. The church has to be rebuilt after each earthquake, but the foun-

dation blocks are as tight as ever.

The Incas were great road builders. They laid paved roads from Ecuador to Chile and from the mountain slopes to the Pacific. Typically five feet wide, the Inca roads are made of smooth rock slabs—sturdy enough pavement that much of it is in perfect condition today. It curls around 65-degree mountain precipices, supported by well-drained stone walls. It has steps where the grades are steep and, where necessary, tunnels through solid rock. When Pizarro arrived, thousands of miles of paved roads lay waiting for the invention of the wheel.

The Incas were daring bridge builders. They liked to live high, like eagles (Cuzco, for exam-

The American Museum of Natural History

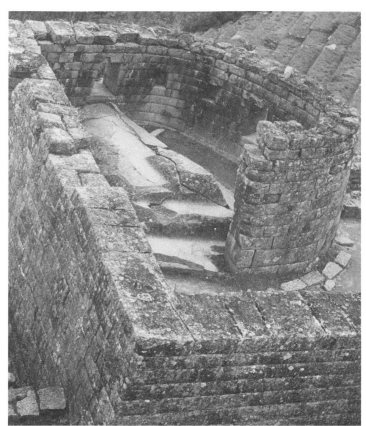

Marie J. Mattson from Black Star

Stone, quarried from the mountaintop, had to be shaped to fit sophisticated patterns and curvatures. These blocks, some of them weighing many tons, were probably beaten and chipped to approximate shape with flint or stone tools, scraping and abrasive grinding, using sand mixtures.

ple, is above 10,000 feet), apparently because every venture into the valleys ended in warfare with less civilized local tribes. So they became bridge builders of most magnificent mien, spanning river gorges with 300-foot suspension bridges woven from liana vines. To destroy a bridge meant the death penalty; and this, in a way, contributed to the downfall of the Incas. When the Spaniards were in hot pursuit, it never *occurred* to the Incas to destroy their bridges behind them.

The Bronze Age lingered late in Peru and environs, but Inca achievements are impressive nonetheless—not only in architecture and engineering but in medicine, agriculture, and animal husbandry as well:

It is estimated that the Incas domesticated more food and medicinal plants than any other people of the time. For example, they found a pea-sized edible tuber high in the Andes and cultivated it into what is now known as the Irish potato. After 300 years and two major famines, Europeans discovered the value of the potato, and today there are Sherpas in highest Nepal living on the same plant (they got it from the British Embassy garden).

The Incas also developed the sweet potato, which they called the *cumara*. Today it is cultivated all over the Polynesian islands, from Hawaii to New Zealand, and it still has roughly the name the Incas gave it: *Kumara* or *Kumala*.

The Incas long recognized the value of ferti-

Courtesy of the Organization of American States

lizer, and certain offshore guano-producing bird islands were allocated to various provinces. It was forbidden to visit these islands during mating season; and it meant the death penalty to kill even *one* of the hundreds of thousands of guano-producing birds.

Masters at domesticating animals, the Incas tamed a small, hard-to-catch Andean rodent called the *cuy*. Today it's known as the guinea pig, although it does not come from Guinea and is not a pig. Even today when an unexpected guest arrives at an Indian home in Peru, the friendly little creatures are scooped off the floor and made into cuy stew—acclaimed as a delicacy by the most sophisticated gourmets.

The Incas also domesticated two species of the wild American camel—the coarse-haired llama as a beast of burden, and the silky-haired alpaca for its fine wool.

Under the conquistadors, the demise of the Incas was tragically swift. The original conquest was made by barely 200 men, but they were aided by an Inca civil war, by the terrifying sight of the huge Spanish horses, and by the crack-of-doom sound of Spanish firearms.

The final blow was struck by the Spanish viceroy Francisco de Toledo. To avenge the murder of an ambassador and a priest, and in a last frantic search for gold, he ordered his soldiers in total pursuit of the Inca emperor Tupac Amaru. They caught him in the Amazon jungle, returned him to Cuzco, and executed him—along with his entire family. Thus, in 1571, less than 40 years after the conquistadors arrived, the last Inca emperor died, and the great civilization sank to its knees for all time.

The conquistadors took many things from the Incas: their land, their freedom, their religion, their gold, their lives. But the ghosts of the Incas may be laughing last. They never yielded Machu Picchu. And they gave the conquistadors one more prize of conquest than they bargained for. The Spaniards returned home not only with Peruvian gold but also with Europe's first major infusion of syphilis.

Marie J. Mattson from Black Star

Remnants of a civilization brilliantly fashioned out of an almost impossible environment. The Incas crisscrossed their mountain slopes with roads, bridges, aqueducts, and complex irrigation systems to cultivate crops that they were the first to domesticate.

Courtesy of the Organization of American States

67

THE CUCKOO CONSTRUCTION COMPANY

How to design a home when the most important thing you'll ever own is an egg

With a spare, muscular body, a strong heart, perfect digestion, rich blood, and incredibly vigorous metabolism, a bird has no excuse for being less than an energetic builder. And given his need for a safe, soft, warm, protective residence in which to conduct a precarious hatching and raising of children, the bird has ample incentive to build the perfect nest. Add 150 million years of evolution to develop the instincts of construction (the beaver has had less than one million), the same eons for natural selection to weed out defective nest-building techniques, and the practice-makes-perfect benefits of having to structure a new home every year—add it all up, and you might expect somewhere to find the equivalent of Gold-Finch Gothic, Bluebird Baroque, Redstart Renaissance, or Warbler Williamsburg.

The Ruby-Throated Hummingbird is one of many species that use lichens to glue their nests onto tree branches. Other varieties of Hummingbird have other adhesives. *Panterpe insignis* of Costa Rica sticks pieces of moss together with the help of spider webs.

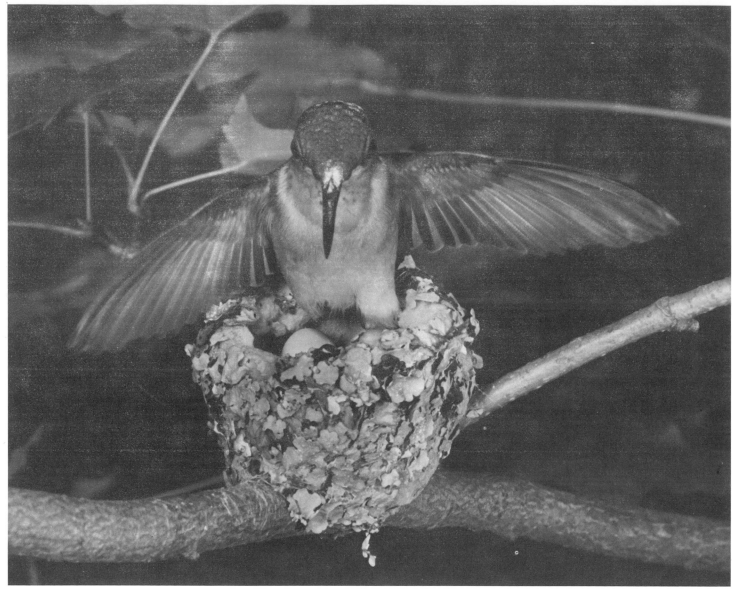

Karl H. Maslowski from Photo Researchers

It didn't work out that way. Nature is awesome in many respects but not all. The ostrich is one of several birds that can't fly. The chicken stays out in the rain and drowns. The squirrel forgets where he buried his nuts. And when it comes to nest building, it would have to be said that in many cases Aves doesn't try hard enough.

The grouse scratches out a little dirt, pulls in a few leaves, and lays its eggs in this shallow depression completely accessible to predators.

The yellow-billed cuckoo makes a skimpy platform of twigs and straw so haphazardly thatched that the eggs occasionally plummet right through it. Some birds hardly even make an attempt. The band-tailed pigeon, whose single white egg would seem to deserve high priority protection, either throws together a loose, jackstraw assembly of twigs or ignores even that formality and lays the egg on the forest floor. The English kestrel will settle for an abandoned crow's nest. And the cowbird simply lays her eggs in other birds' nests and leaves the hatching to them.

In fairness to birds and in quaking respect for bird-lovers, it should be conceded that avians do tend to build roughly what they need. If the resident is weatherproof, the house needn't be. Nests are for nesting, for incubation and feeding—for eggs and their occupants—and in accommodating this cargo, birds' nests reveal a construction code of their own.

The essential rule is deceptively simple; namely, that lopsided eggs are laid in shallow nests.

Since eggs vary in shape, they differ in the distance they are likely to roll if jarred by a parent, predator, or a gust of wind. An egg that is much larger on one end than the other will roll in a very tight circle. One that is close to a regular oval shape is likely to roll farther and could more easily be nudged clear out of the nest. So for nearly all species of birds, the rule of thumb is the rule of egg: birds who lay lopsided eggs build shallow nests, while birds who lay nearly symmetrical eggs build deeper nests to hold them.

Aside from keeping the eggs intact, this principle may be necessary for proper hatching. There have been experiments to show that the eggs must be touching each other if they are to hatch at roughly the same time (and if they don't, the parent has a nasty dilemma: how to sit on the remaining eggs without sitting on the babies already hatched). Some researchers have reported scratching sounds inside the eggs, infrequent at first and then speeding up as hatching time approaches. If the eggs are in contact, these sounds tend to synchronize, and the embryos develop toward emergence at the same pace. Although lopsided eggs would tend to remain in contact even in a shallow nest, a deeper cavity might be necessary to keep oval eggs in touch with each other.

Of course some species go well beyond the "rule of egg" in the sophistication of their nest building techniques. Of the 30,000 or so varieties of birds, here are a few of the more interesting architects and engineers.

There are Eurasian Bitterns, True Bitterns, and Black Mangrove Bitterns. Last and, alas, least is the Least Bittern, smallest of this far-flung family of wading birds related to the heron. The Least Bittern resides by shallow waters, where it grapples its nest to reed stalks and sometimes tangles the reed tops together to form a rude thatched roof over the nest.

(Top, left) one of the best builders in the hawk family, the Red Shoulder likes sturdy structurals but is not averse to fluffy embellishments. Small branches, sticks, and twigs form a strong, shallow platform, lined inside with soft bark, lichens, moss, and pine and hemlock sprigs. Decorations include bits of white plant down, strips of bark, and leaves.

(Top, right) locked in the DNA of the Red-Eyed Vireo is the blueprint for this basket-shaped structure. Siding: a sturdy weave of bark strips and wood for the warp, paper and plant down for the woof. Furnishings: a soft lining of bark fiber, vine tendrils, and pine needles. Trim: ornamental cocoons and fragments of wasp nests.

(Bottom, left) the renowned Baltimore Oriole and assorted kin construct intricately woven hanging or semihanging nests out of dried grasses and, in the case of the Baltimore, yarn, string, or any available fiber.

(Bottom, right) Silvery plant fiber, delicate grasses and bark shreds make a thick, strong, but beautiful nest for the Yellow Warbler. Its deeply cupped down-lined cavity sometimes becomes a two-story affair: if a Cowbird lays an egg in the nest, the Warbler builds a new floor over it and leaves it unhatched while the Warbler eggs are tended on the second floor.

To hear a bird make its nest, it is necessary to turn to the Woodpeckers, Flickers, and Sapsuckers, who hammer tree trunks with sharp, chisel-shaped beaks to carve out nesting holes or alcoves. One subspecies, the California or Ant-Eating Woodpecker, drills two feet into a white oak or sycamore, whether or not he needs a nest. If not, he fills the hole with acorns.

Shown here is a Pileated Woodpecker—who obviously *did* need a nest—and a Red-Shafted Flicker, who isn't telling.

Allan D. Cruickshank from National Audubon Society. Collection/Photo Researchers.

Karl H. Maslowski from National Audubon Society Collection/Photo Researchers

74

Hal. H. Harrison from National Audubon Society Collection/Photo Researchers

The principles of reinforced concrete and fiber-reinforced plastics are relatively new to man but millions of years old to the Barn Swallow. The mud outer walls of his nest are strengthened by grass and straw fiber reinforcement.

(Top) here is the bird that literally drools his nest. The East Indian Swift dwells in a shell of his own solidified saliva. Repulsive? Not to the Swift, and not to the people who use his nest to make bird's nest soup.

(Bottom) the Ovenbird gets its name from the brick oven shape of its nest. North American varieties build the nest of leaves and grassy weeds, usually on or near the ground. It has a side entrance, a roof, and a light overhang of leaves or underbrush as camouflage. The Red Ovenbird of South America builds a clay structure of roughly the same shape.

Along the Amazon, the Japim weaves his socklike nest out of tropical grasses and suspends the entire assemblage from a branch.

Jen and Des Bartlett from Photo Researchers

The sparrowlike weaverbird family includes some of the most accomplished roof-thatchers in the business. The masked weaver (right) interlaces what looks like a ball of kite string. The red-billed weaver (above) with its hanging thatch nests colonizes some sections of the African savanna so thickly as to become an agricultural pest. Its near relative, the social weaverbird of southwest Africa, may have taught early man how to build grass huts— showing the way with big apartment houses in the Acacia trees, topped by umbrella-shaped thatched grass roofs.

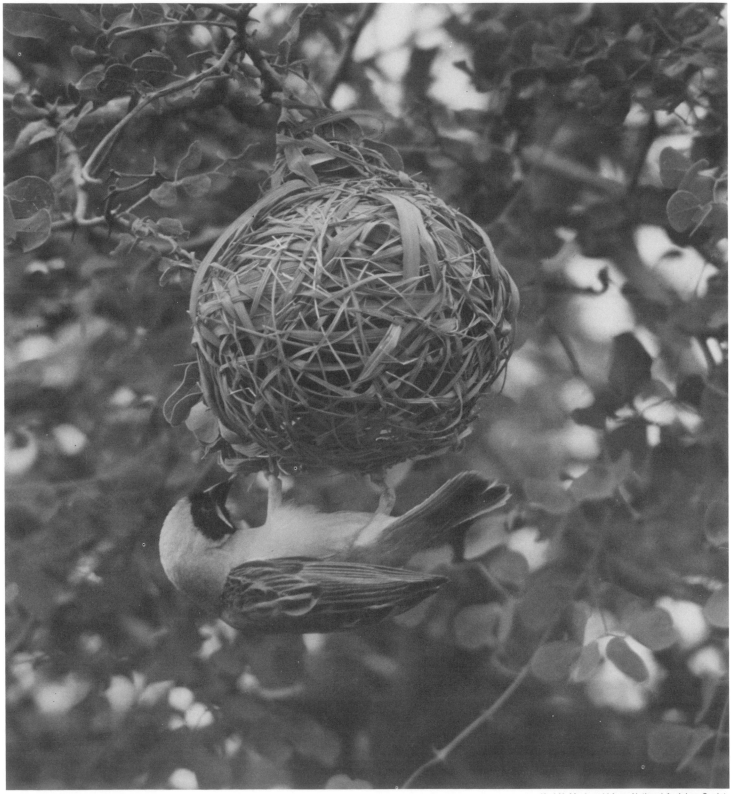

Karl H. Maslowski from National Audubon Society
Collection/Photo Researchers

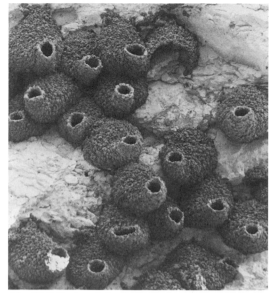

Condominiums, Cliff Swallow style. Mud chambers are shaped like gourds or flasks, attached to cliff faces or caked under the eaves of buildings. The Cliff Swallow's main comfort requirement seems to be the presence of a great many Cliff Swallows. In the nest itself, only a few feathers and a little grass are used as lining.

PETRA

**Match me such marvel, save in Eastern clime,
A rose-red city, half as old as time.**

From the sonnet "Petra" by John W. Burgon

In crudest terms, there are two ways to make a building: take pieces of stone or wood or something comparable and stack or fasten them together, or find a piece of rock somewhat larger than the finished structure is planned to be and hollow it out.

The hollowing method requires uncommon patience and boulders of such uncommon size that building sites are hard to find. A few times it has happened: once in the Arabian desert, at the city of Petra, and that site was so hard to find that for a thousand years the city was simply lost.

George Holton from Photo Researchers

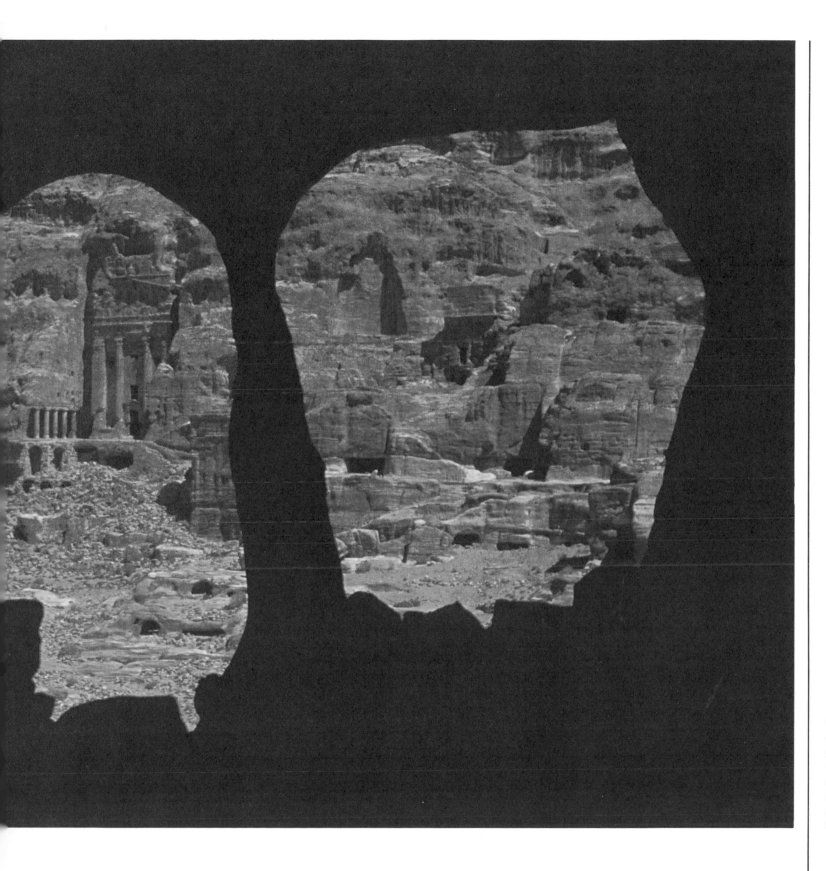

Virtually as inaccessible today as they were two thousand years ago, the tombs of Petra rise out of the faces of rock cliffs in the Arabian desert. Here, the Palace Tomb, built during the rule of Roman colonial governors, is seen from a cave dating from the earlier Nabataean period.

79

Courtesy of Historisches Museum, Basel

Midway between the Dead Sea and the Gulf of Aqaba in Jordan, Petra is surrounded by jagged rock cliffs. It is all but inaccessible and almost perfectly camouflaged; from the outside, nothing is visible but a forbidding range of craggy mountains. What it took to rediscover Petra was an adventurous Swiss aristocrat, disguised as a Bedouin, who was able to allay the suspicions of local Arabs and enter the hidden valley on the pretext of wishing to sacrifice a goat.

That was in 1812, when Johann Ludwig Burckhardt became the first European since the time of the Romans to see Petra and return to tell about it. Once a flourishing caravan center, the city had dwindled in influence, finally fell silent sometime before the seventh century, and was soon forgotten by the world—except

for a small Arab tribe who believed in legends of great hidden wealth and guarded the secret and the treasure as theirs.

Burckhardt had not heard those legends. He was not looking for treasure or for Petra. He was merely roving the Middle East to learn Arab languages and customs so that he could later explore for the British African Association in North Africa. In Bedouin sheepskin and headdress, he tried to melt into the regional populace, but with imperfect success: three times desert sheikhs offered him their protection for a fee, then had him robbed and left in the wilderness. Each time he dragged himself back to Damascus—a little tougher, a little wiser.

On his fourth venture Burckhardt set a zigzag course for Cairo. Camped near the village

80

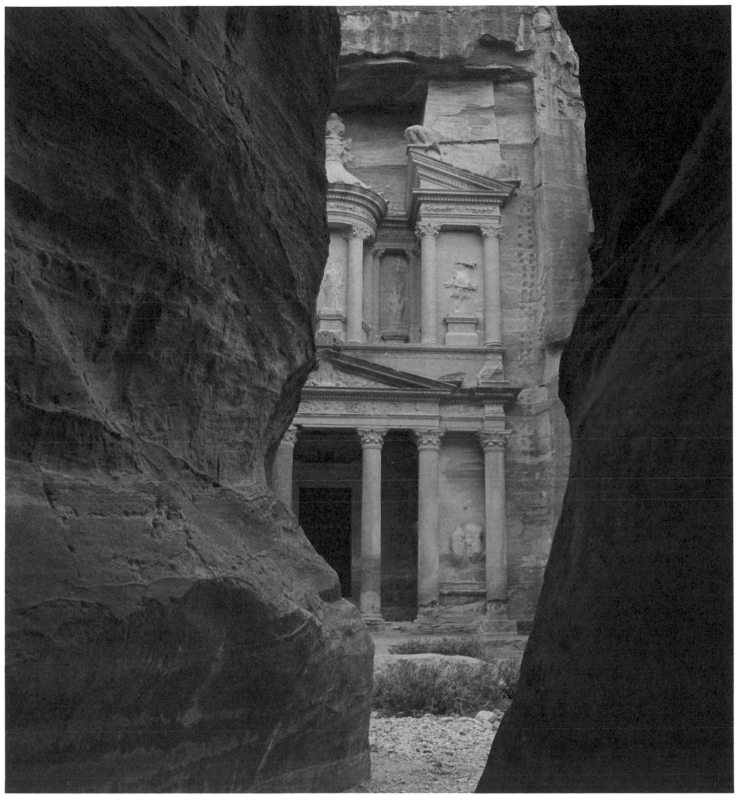

Petra is reached today by the same path that Burckhardt followed through a narrow, boulder-strewn canyon. First glimpse of the hidden city from the darkness of the canyon is the Khaznah, the "Treasury of the Pharoah."

George Holton from Photo Researchers

81

One of the structures dating from Roman times reveals the spectacular sandstone strata of the cliff face out of which it is carved. The coloration of these patterns shifts during the day with the changing angles of the sun.

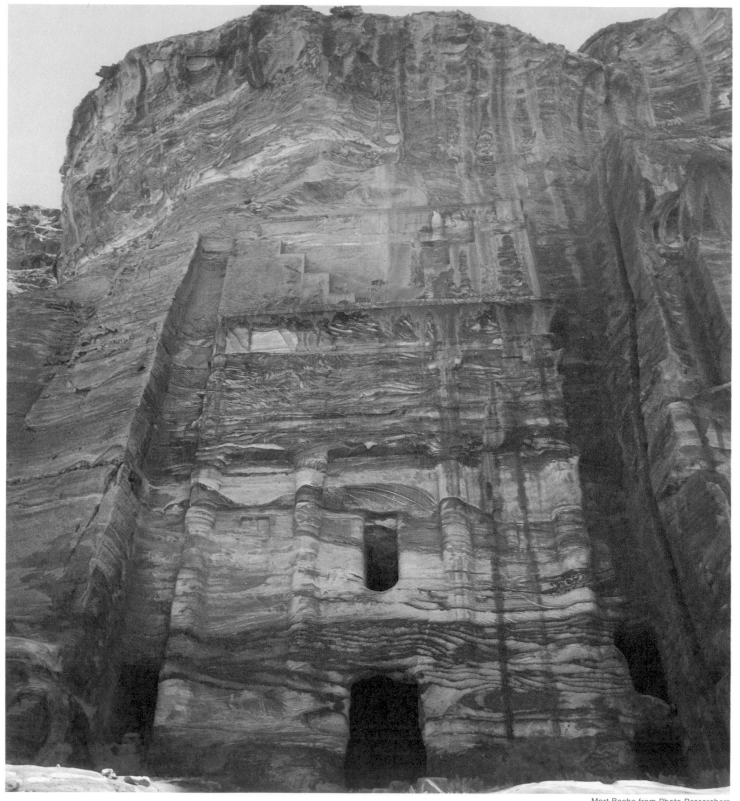

of Alji at Wadi Musa—the Valley of Moses— he took advantage of his hard-won linguistics to learn that there were ruins nearby, including the tomb of Aaron, brother of Moses. Incurably curious, Burckhardt recruited a guide, somehow convincing the Arab of his fervent wish to sacrifice a goat at Aaron's tomb.

For Burckhardt, as for the visitor today, the route into Petra was a trip back through time. Down from the village he rode along the foot of steep, impenetrable slopes until his guide pointed to a narrow cleft where a stream entered the range of cliffs.

If the guide had been suspicious at first, it was Burckhardt who grew wary as the gorge (called the Sik) deepened and narrowed. Between rock faces over 200 feet high, they picked their way through an eerie, boulder-strewn canyon over a mile long, until it squeezed to a width of less than twenty feet and seemed about to dead-end in darkness.

Then, through the narrow cleft ahead, Burck-

hardt glimpsed the sight that has stunned travelers ever since: a magnificent temple over a hundred feet high, its intricate facade of columns, capitals, statues, pediments, and entablatures carved out of the vertical rock face and almost perfectly preserved for close to 2,000 years. Brilliant in sunlight on the far wall of a transverse gorge, this massive mausoleum is called the Khaznah, "Treasury of the Pharaoh." It is only the beginning.

Past the Khaznah, there are small family sepulchres and large royal tombs, all carefully hewn from the sandstone cliff faces. Where the gorge widens there is a theater large enough for two to three thousand spectators, its curving benches carved from rock strata of the canyon floor. Finally the great stone corridor opens onto a broad, enclosed valley nearly a mile square, and there is Petra.

Its most awesome wonders are natural. Incredible rock walls tower 600 feet above the valley. Surreal patterns of sandstone texture

H. Schreider from Photo Researchers

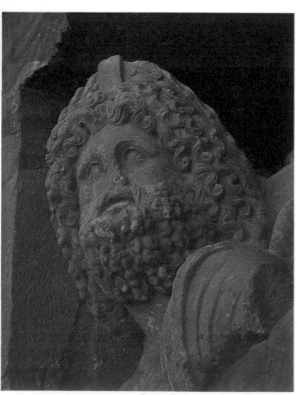

and strata trace great eddies and swirls that alter in hue and brilliance from hour to hour with the traversing sun. And color is everywhere: a bewildering interplay of red, orange, blue, gray, yellow, brown, purple, pink, white, and black. Reds predominate, but virtually no tint of the spectrum has gone unreflected by Petra's varying stone.

Once the capital and impregnable stronghold of the Nabataeans, Petra covered its slopes with temples, palaces, baths, private houses, and tombs—everywhere, tombs—interconnected by a paved road that followed the meanderings of Wadi Musa. Stone staircases twist precariously up the slopes to the "high places" where stone altars received animal sacrifices to several generations of gods. There are at least eleven of these high places, most equipped with trenches to receive the blood and with water tanks, fireplaces, and stone seating for worshippers.

The active life of the city reached from about five centuries before Christ to five centuries after—roughly the span of Rome. The earliest known occupants were the Edomites referred to in the Old Testament, followed by the Nabataeans and the Romans. Finally there was a restoration of Arab rule. The ancient Greeks made at least one abortive military conquest of Petra, and contact between the two cultures continued. Caravans from India, Persia, Egypt, the interior of Arabia, and the maritime cities of Syria and Palestine added to Petra's rich mixture of custom, culture, and architecture.

The Nabataeans soon developed a hybrid architectural style, distilled chiefly from Greek and Assyrian patterns and characterized by the use of stepped pinnacles. Later buildings evidence increasing Roman influence: larger, more imposing tomb facades, rows of columns, and replacement of the stepped pinnacle by triangular pediments.

Tombs are everywhere, throughout the city and studding the surrounding cliffs. The niches of this cave are presumed to have been burial chambers.

Interior chambers were hollowed out, leaving columns, alcoves, and decorative detail, just as if they had been constructed of masonry rather than sculpted in place. No one knows what sort of metal tools were used for this prodigious reshaping of the valley's sandstone.

The Khaznah seems to mingle Roman and Hellenistic features, and a few structures—like the large mausoleum known as the Palace Tomb—are out-and-out Roman imitations, erected under the rule of colonial governors in the first two or three centuries A.D.

On every side are structures and public works whose execution is difficult to imagine. Four ancient obelisks stand twenty-three feet high on the south side of the wadi: the artistic and religious remains of a massive rock hill that was entirely carved away except for these four slender shafts, still rooted in mother rock. A huge tunnel, 30 feet high and 40 feet wide, bores 300 feet through solid stone just to serve as a storm sewer during infrequent heavy rains. Spring-fed the rest of the year, Petra is ribbed with channels carved in stone to conduct

the water and with huge cisterns to store it. One of these channels carried water from a spring in the upper wadi through the Sik, where Moses is said to have drawn forth a spring by striking a rock.

At this date no one knows what metal tools were used to hollow out the large cubical chambers of Petra's tombs and temples. Many of these rooms are designed to fit under black strata of rock, which are denser and harder than other layers of the sandstone, forming safe, durable ceilings. In the Khaznah the central chamber is forty feet square; two flanking chambers are each close to thirty feet on a side; and all three have smaller rooms or niches carved into their walls.

Probably the most ambitious construction project in the history of Petra—and certainly

The most ambitious project in Petra is the 130-foot-high Dair, or Monastery (left), which was carved nearly 600 feet above the city on one of the peaks that ring the mile-square valley (right).

one of the greatest whittling jobs in the history of anybody—was the conversion of a mountain top into the structure that Arabs called *ad-Dair* or *ad-Deir*, the Monastery (which it was not).

Carved from a massive peak of gray sandstone, the Dair stands 130 feet high and nearly 600 feet above the city. To hew it out of the mountain the Nabataeans had first to cut away a jutting cliff, leaving a stone mass over 150 feet wide and nearly that high from which to sculpt the structure itself, and a broad area in front, which they leveled for an esplanade. Probably a temple rather than a tomb, the Dair is heavily Roman in design. Eight enormous columns support a pediment and eight more rise from there to frame a second story, centered by an immense urn atop a miniature temple complete with dome. All from one rock.

Niches and porches of the Dair, obviously intended for statuary, are now empty, their stone inhabitants carried off centuries ago. Throughout the city and its surrounding slopes, the tombs, temples, dwellings, and high places of worship have been stripped of their statues, icons, and urns, despite stern warnings on memorial inscriptions:

> May Dushara and Manuthu and Quishah curse everyone who shall sell this tomb or buy it or frame for it any writ. The tomb and this its inscription are inviolable things, after the manner of the Nabataeans, for ever and ever.

What *did* prove inviolable, except for the gradual erosion of wind-driven sand and rain, are the essential structures of the city itself—too large to steal and too sturdy to smash because they were carved from solid petra, which, like Peter, means *rock*.

HIGH GOTHIC

**On Ascension Thursday
the church fell down**

For four years the tallest building in the world stood in the small French town of Beauvais, between Paris and Amiens. There, from 1569 to 1573, an unfinished cathedral stretched heavenward, its vault surpassing that of any other Gothic cathedral before or since, its spire rising higher than St. Peter's in Rome, higher by nearly twenty feet than the great pyramid of Cheops, higher than anything, anywhere, and higher than its structural underpinnings could long support. The Cathedral of St. Pierre at Beauvais is still standing. It lacks a spire; it lacks a nave. But it has a massive, magnificent choir and apse, an exceptional clock, and a strange, sad story of construction.

A cathedral without a spire marks the
site where, for four years, four
hundred years ago, the little French
town of Beauvais could boast the
tallest building on earth.
Paul Almasy

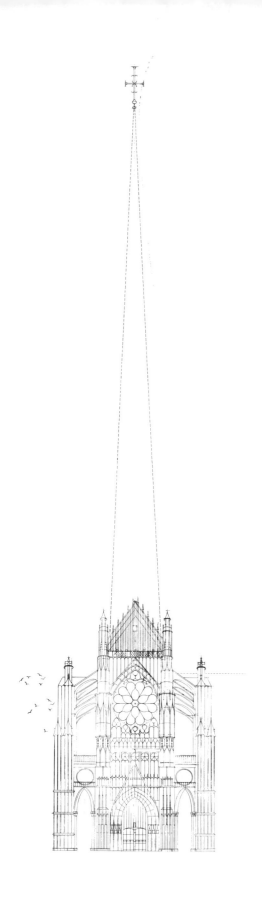

It was cathedral-building time in France when St. Pierre was begun. During the twelfth and thirteenth centuries, a wave of church building unlike anything else in history spread through medieval Europe. France alone fostered at least 600 cathedrals and major churches and 500 abbeys between the years 1170 and 1270, and lowly was the town without a large church, or at least the beginnings of one.

Ahead lay the fourteenth, possibly the worst century yet counted by European man. Still further ahead, the rationalist eighteenth century would look back unsympathetically to the time of the great church building, would regard it as barbaric, and would slur it with the name "Gothic." Yet, it was the great synthesis of the Middle Ages, the period that tied each man, his society, and his religion together, and expressed these combined aspirations in stone pulled to unprecedented heights.

Midway in the period, in the year 1225, Milon de Nanteuil, Bishop of Beauvais, ordered construction to begin on a new diocesan cathedral. In addition to its spiritial needs, both the pride and the prosperity of Beauvais were at stake. Only thirty miles away, Amiens was erecting the nave and west facade of a cathedral that its builders boasted would be the tallest and most beautiful in France. Since major cathedrals drew thousands of pilgrims each year, economics alone might have been enough to prompt Beauvais to match its sister city and the hundreds of other French towns then busy with their buildings.

Paul Almasy

The choir vaulting of St. Pierre-Beauvais (left) soars to an awesome 157 feet. The floor plan (below) shows the cathedral's choir, apse, and transept. It lacks the usual nave, or central hall, which would ordinarily have been built first and would have given broader structural support to the spire.

Paul Almasy

So construction began, but it did not, in the usual sequence of things, begin with the nave: that would unnecessarily delay the point, the towering spire that was planned to exceed the height of anything in Christendom. A small tenth-century Romanesque church was left standing on the site of the nave, while work was started on the apse and choir on which the spire would eventually rest. Year by year the mighty structure rose until, a half-century after its plan had been announced, the apse and choir stood complete, twenty feet higher than the nave of Amiens and forty feet higher than Chartres.

The ambulatory (the walkway around the semicircular apse, from which seven chapels radiated) was pulled from the usual one-story height to a stupendous three stories. The triforium and clerestory above the inner aisle of the choir matched this lofty level, and the choir vaults hovered an incredible 157 feet above the pavement, braced by two flights of flying buttresses. Even without its spire St. Pierre was the marvel of France.

In 1284 the vaults collapsed. Possibly the foundation was insufficiently solid to support such massive weight. More likely, ambition had outrun engineering, and the thrust and counter-

Paul Almasy

With or without a spire to point the way, arcades furnished with benches make the cloister at St. Pierre a pleasant place for spiritual contemplation and study.

thrust of uncommonly high arches had been miscalculated. As the choir was laboriously repaired, additional piering was added; however, before the town and the diocese could muster the courage and the funds to proceed with further construction, a full two hundred years would pass.

A *very* full two hundred years. The calamitous fourteenth century devastated Europe with war, disease, civil disorder, and social dissolution. The Hundred Years' War bled the youth and wealth of France and England. The Black Death struck in the 1340s and left many regions with less than half their people still alive. What

trade routes and pilgrimage routes had not been closed by war were choked off by pestilence. Towns languished; taxation soared; community and family life withered; the political and religious unity of the Holy Roman Empire began to disintegrate. There was no money for cathedrals, little will to build them, no guiding philosophy or purpose or design to shape them.

By the time work was resumed at Beauvais Renaissance architecture had produced the Rayonnant movement, which took the soaring verticals of the Gothic and experimented with stretching them as thinly and delicately as pos-

After a two-hundred-year delay, work on the cathedral resumed during the sixteenth century under the direction of Martin Chambiges. Intricate tracery added during this period reflects an intervening shift to the *Flamboyant* phase of Gothic design.

sible, and the Flamboyant movement, named for the flame shapes it used in panes of glass and tracery. Both influences appeared in the final work on St. Pierre—Beauvais. Intricate Flamboyant facades grace the transepts, whose design was begun in 1500 by the renowned master Martin Chambiges and carried forward by Jean Vast and Michael Lalye. By 1548, both the north and south transepts were complete. There were still no plans for a nave, but discussions were already underway on design of the final triumph, the crossing tower.

In 1558, as the drum for Michelangelo's dome on St. Peter's was taking shape in Rome, Beauvais began its second bid for preeminence. Its new crossing spire would surpass St. Peter's 450-foot dome by a full forty feet. For eleven years the dream inched upward to its pinnacle: three stories of stone, one of oak, and an iron cross in the sky, 497 feet above the ground.

From the first, exultation in the town was mixed with concern. Suggestions were made for additional pierage and nave bays to stabilize support, and for replacing the heavy cross atop the spire with a lighter one. Finally, in the spring of 1573, masons were engaged to reinforce the tower's supporting columns. But it was too late.

On Ascension day the congregation attended services and began to leave the church. Only a few stragglers remained when an ominous scattering of dust and small stones filtered down from the upper reaches of the vault. Then, with a terrifying crack, the spire's supporting columns collapsed and, in five seconds, Beauvais had not the tallest but the shortest of all major Gothic cathedrals.

Gloom hung over the town. Even worse, jagged fragments of the spire hung precariously from a 200-foot stump and from edges of the

As seen in this detail of a wood sculpture, resumption of work in the sixteenth century brought lavish ornamentation to the interior as well as the exterior.

Paul Almasy

damaged roof, threatening lethal showers of rubble into the square; and workmen refused the suicidal job of clearing the remains so that repairs could begin. The wreckage of Beauvais' cathedral was destined to make only one man happy: a criminal awaiting execution in the town prison won his freedom by climbing to the spire and detaching the dangling remains.

Half a church stands today in Beauvais, where visitors can see an awesome, if incomplete, triumph of High Gothic. In 1929 one such visitor, author Sydney Clark, took particular note of an elaborate astronomical clock in the cathedral choir. Standing forty feet high, alive with 90,000 parts manipulating 52 dials, the great clock ticks off days, weeks, months, even the age of the Earth. Clark checked this age (5,730 years) through its biblical references and found that not only architecture but also time was out of joint at Beauvais. Its clock solemnly proclaimed the year to be A.D. 1726.

Despite its manifest difficulty, the building of the Beauvais Cathedral was not impossible. Some historians argue that the plans would have been perfectly practical if the architects had been blessed with better materials, such as good, hard stone, plus better financing and more capable help. The architects of St. Pierre—Beauvais had an additional problem: how to maintain control of a project that might require four or five hundred years to complete. Presumably the original designer would not have allowed construction of a spire that depended for support on a nonexistent nave. Cologne Cathedral, with proportions close to those of St. Pierre—Beauvais was left unfinished in the thirteenth century; but Cologne was completed in the nineteenth century, showing that St. Pierre could have been successfully engineered.

96

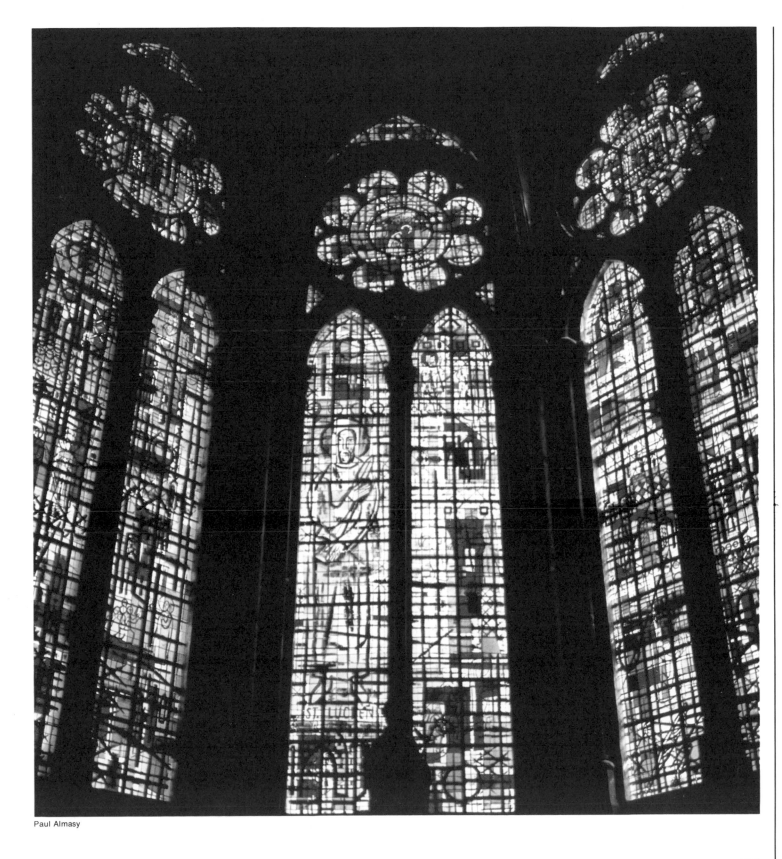

Paul Almasy

When a church can't keep its stone intact, what hope is there for windows? Modern stained glass has replaced the original panes, the last of which were lost to bombings in 1940.

97

THE GREAT WALL OF CHINA

The raising of the wall

There is considerable evidence that the Chinese Emperor Ch'in Shih Huang-ti inadvertently toppled the Roman Empire. When his Great Wall discouraged the Huns from attacking China to the south, they turned west and invaded Europe, starting a six-century chain reaction that ultimately brought Attila to the gates of Rome. Had the Great Wall spanned the Urals instead of skirting the Mongolian plains, today's maps might show a different world entirely.

Rene Burri from Magnum

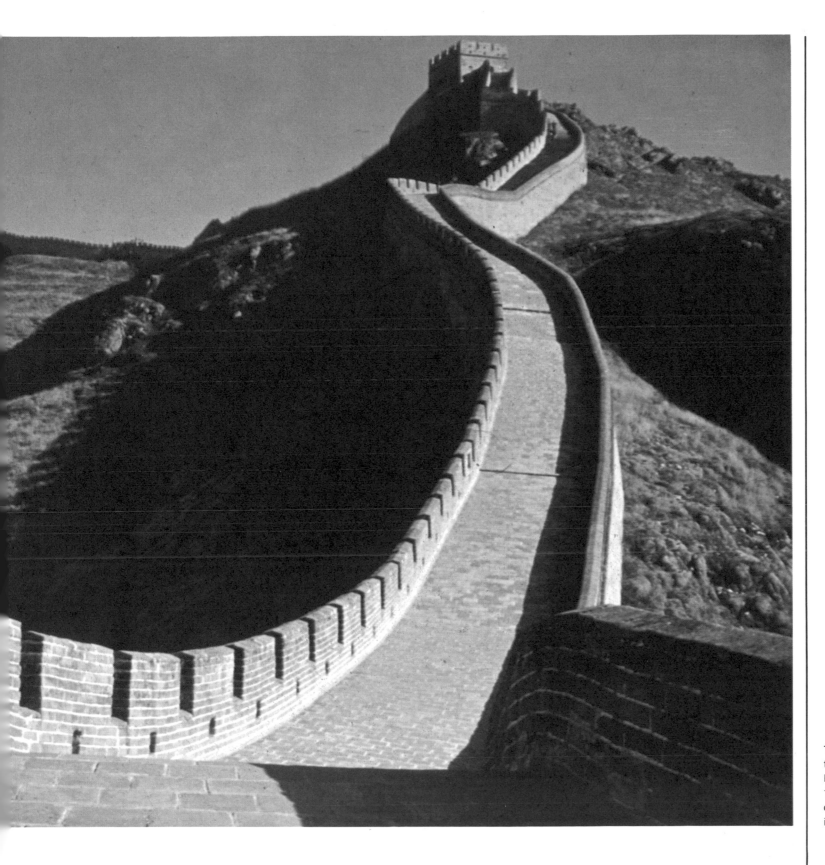

The walls of northern China became the Great Wall of China around 200 B.C., when Ch'in Shih Huang Ti had 1,200 miles of fortifications built to connect the various sections already in place.

The wall was one of Ch'in's two great obsessions. The other was immortality. He erased China's history by burning its books so that he could be known as the first emperor.

The fact that the wall is where it is proceeds first from an age-old Chinese preoccupation with walls and, second, from the febrile ambition of Ch'in Shih Huang-ti. Ch'in aspired to nothing less than immortality. He ordered the burning of all the books in China except scientific texts and his own memoirs. He annointed himself the first emperor and claimed divine stature. He banished his mother (for a first emperor who is also a god, it is awkward to have a mother), and he searched ceaselessly for an elixir that would grant him eternal life. And, about 221 B.C., he launched the one enterprise that is still reaching for eternity: the Great Wall of China.

Ch'in had brought the warring states of China brutally to heel and was making plans for establishing a true empire, including uniform laws, currency, and weights and measures; a system of highways; and an end of feudal land holdings. To prevent barbarian incursions into his grand design, he ordered that various defensive walls along the northern boundary be connected into one immense fortification.

The emperor assigned the task to his commander-in-chief, Meng T'ien, and told him to hurry. Mindful of Ch'in's penchant for decapitating those who obeyed imperfectly, Meng hurried. He conscripted and relocated almost

The Great Wall is composed of two side walls, twenty-five to thirty feet apart, made of granite blocks topped with fire-clay bricks. The space between is filled and paved with brick to form a roadway, flanked with parapets, with watchtowers every 100 to 400 yards.

Rene Burri from Magnum

Bruno Barbey from Magnum

The basic design of the Great Wall remained the same whether it cut through mountains or crossed the open plains. But on the plains, instead of granite, the construction material was sun-baked loess, a clay which tended to erode over the centuries. Roughly 1,500 miles of history's greatest fortification are still standing, admired now by tourists rather than generals.

an entire generation of Chinese manpower. To feed a construction crew numbering 1,500,000, he placed thirty-four supply dumps along the course of the wall. What provisions were not stolen in transit were lost to one of China's worst vermin plagues, but Meng pushed ahead.

By its description his construction site was a nightmare. The Chinese army, like all armies, wanted the high ground. Through mountainous terrain, Meng had his workmen chisel two parallel furrows, often out of solid rock. From these trenches, twenty-five to thirty feet apart, they built the main walls on massive footers of granite blocks, piled four to five feet wide and from six to twelve feet high. These were topped by outer walls of large fired-clay bricks, two feet thick, in what may have been the first large-scale use of this building material.

At their tops the outer walls were about twenty feet apart and from eighteen to thirty feet high. Between them, workmen dumped earth, rock, and clay, trampled this filler with their feet, and probably tamped it with logs. By most accounts, the core material also contained the thousands of laborers who died during construction. Finally a brick platform was built over the top to provide an elevated road.

Flanking this narrow cartway were crenellated parapets that doubled as guardrails and as protection for defending archers and spearmen. And rising another twenty feet from the top of the wall were uncounted watchtowers— *literally* uncounted, but there were at least 10,000 towers on the wall and perhaps as many as 25,000—one every 100 to 400 yards.

When its course left the mountains for the

Rene Burri from Magnum

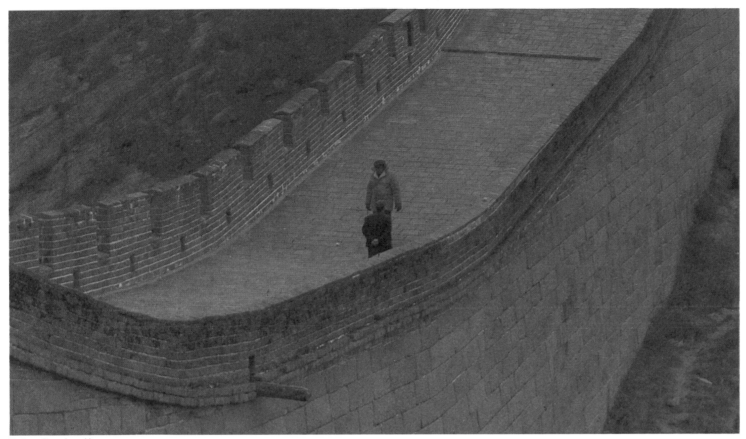

Barbara Dane from Magnum

Construction of the wall took ten years and 1,500,000 laborers, many thousands of whom died of these rigors and were buried in the wall itself. The wall had at least 10,000 watchtowers and more than enough masonry to build two million houses.

open plains, the wall retained its basic design, but construction methods changed. Workmen dug the same parallel trenches but saved the dirt, which contained a high percentage of a yellowish, calcareous substance called loess. Meng had wooden forms built to frame the outer walls. When the loess was rammed into these forms and a little water added, it stiffened and baked in the sun to form a hard, dry wall. Some of this loess surface was faced with brick, but much of it was left bare, to be gradually worn away by centuries of wind from the deserts.

All told Ch'in added at least 1,200 miles of wall to existing structures. With later additions in the Ming dynasty, the Great Wall reached a length of 2,500 zigzag miles, spanning a 1,500-mile frontier. One historian who visited the wall around 1800 calculated that it contained more masonry than all of the nearly two million houses in England and Scotland. Ch'in's portion was completed in an incredible ten years, at a cost in human life that has been estimated at more than a million men.

Ch'in had little use for scholars, and scholars have had little use for him. One of the kindest things ever said about him was that he ruined one generation of Chinese to save many generations. His wall, though it didn't prevent invasions, certainly delayed them and reduced their number. And if Ch'in failed to find the elixir to cheat death, he succeeded in cheating obscurity. He is remembered as the man who burned the books and is memorialized by the hundreds of miles that remain of the Great Wall. He also had a country named after him—China.

IGLOOS

How to build a northern hemisphere

There is no practical way to take an accurate census of Eskimos, but best estimates see roughly 50,000 of them scattered over a geographic region 3,200 miles long — all of it cold.

The arrival first of traders, then prospectors, military contingents, research stations, and finally oil drillers and pipeline companies could easily cause Eskimo culture to disappear before it is well understood. In many Alaskan and Canadian Eskimo communities, electrical wiring, wooden frame buildings, and snowmobiles have replaced whale oil, igloos, and dogsleds. With a radio in each house and a stereo in the village co-op, young people take up the six-string guitar and ignore the Eskimo skin drum. The igloo becomes not a mainstay residence but a field expedient for camping. Boy Scouts build them, and hunters, and the Canadian Air Force on bivouac.

The American Museum of Natural History

For the Eskimo not yet touched by this creeping encroachment, life is a harsher, more difficult, though possibly more coherent, set of realities. He speaks a complex language, masters an elaborate system of religious belief in which every object is possessed by a spirit, and lives in a primitive commune which intermingles monogamy, polygamy, and polyandry. His architecture, since it is a pure matter of survival, is less complicated.

The Eskimo family has a winter home and a summer home, each made of the building materials that nature provides in season and ready to use. The dwelling for summer may be a tent made of caribou hide, which offers the only physical property required: waterproofing. In winter, depending on the locale, a home may consist of mud and stone; but in regions of unrelenting cold and endless snow it is the snow itself that furnishes thermal insulation and shelter.

For economy, simplicity, and speed of construction, the igloo may never be matched. A man and his wife can build one in an hour, complete with skylight, using no tools other than a simple bone knife. But there is a knack to it.

Not far from prime seal hunting grounds, the Eskimo picks a clear, level spot on the frozen snow and lays out a circle ten to fifteen feet in diameter. Then he carves blocks of snow from within the circle and lays them around the perimeter in an upward spiral, thus excavating and raising walls at the same time. He piles these snow blocks in narrowing circles until he has formed a hemisphere, with an opening left at ground level for access and another near the top.

Into the higher of the two openings he puts a piece of clear ice to serve as a window or skylight. This last piece is a little harder to find, so it's not uncommon for the Eskimo family to

The Eskimo adapts to his environment with admirable economy of effort. In southern subarctic latitudes where part of the year is free of snow, the igloo is often made of sod, dirt, and stone. In colder regions, the Eskimo may have two homes: a tent built on simple frames for the summer and a winter home or seal-hunting shelter made of ice and snow.

Steve McCutcheon

The American Museum of Natural History

109

carry around a choice piece of ice for several weeks before igloo-building time.

Once the snow-block beehive is up, the Eskimo packs every crack with loose snow. Then his wife takes over.

She crawls in through the door opening—which is designed to be just large enough for her but too narrow for, say, a polar bear—and lights a blubber lamp inside. Feeding the lamp constantly with whale oil or seal blubber, she gets a small fire started, then seals the entrance and builds the fire higher.

It isn't long until the entire igloo softens and begins to melt. Because of its hemispherical contour, the water runs down the walls instead of dripping. When the entire structure is damp, she opens the entrance, and the cold blast of Arctic air freezes the walls and welds the structure so solidly that nothing short of the spring thaw can damage it.

Inside, the snow igloo is not only snug but surprisingly well lighted. Aside from the oil lamp or cooking fire and the window of ice, the snow blocks themselves are translucent enough to admit a little sunlight, or even bright moonlight.

Furniture is simple: a three-foot-high snow shelf at the rear, to serve as a family bed. Remaining floor space is left for cooking, eating, and storage, although most of the family provisions are kept in a tunnel—usually about fifteen feet long—built out from the entrance.

In the icebound northernmost regions this building technique has remained unchanged for hundreds of years. The only recent innovation is a questionable one: some Eskimo families have now acquired iron stoves through their limited trading, and the overheated result is often a slowly melting igloo that needs constant bolstering and patching.

Photos, C. Bonington from Woodfin Camp & Associates

As igloo building becomes a vestige of times past rather than a mainstay of residential architecture, its deft art may well deteriorate. Eskimos increasingly abandon this style of shelter while arctic newcomers struggle to master it—in Explorer Scouting programs and survival training courses of the Canadian Air Force. There are two basic methods. Snow blocks can be laid in concentric rings, each course diminishing in diameter as the igloo rises; or, in a more sophisticated technique, the blocks are laid in one, continuous upward spiral.

Notes for the backyard igloo-builder

Temperate-zone urban or suburban igloos require considerable compromise. The structure an Eskimo would be likely to build in Westchester or Evanston would involve several tons of wood, sod, and stone—and the neighborhood children would never accept it as an igloo. Best bet is to ignore the lack of north latitude and build an Arctic snow-block igloo anyway.

Snow blocks may be molded in a wooden box or cut from large, cold-rolled snowballs. For the window a piece of clear polyethylene film can simulate lake ice. You can't use the melt-freeze solidifying process that Eskimos use in subzero temperatures, but you can certainly use a sprinkling can. On a cold day, a little water on the outside of the igloo will do the job, at least well enough for a neighborhood where there is no polar bear to attempt a forced entry.

For at least 30,000 years, survival in harsh northern climates has required the knack of building shelter from the materials at hand. Depending on locale and time of year, an igloo may be made of snow and ice, sod, logs, stone, bone, or animal hides. Sometimes the home becomes permanent.

Photos, Steve McCutcheon

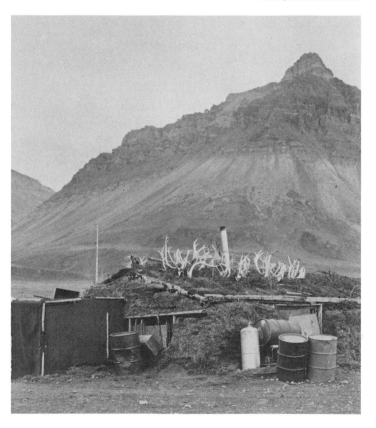

Variations on the theme

Further south, where hard-frozen snow is less abundant and vegetation more plentiful, the construction technology changes. Although snow is often used as an exterior insulation layer, the basic structural materials are various combinations of logs, twigs, driftwood, mud, moss, and stone.

In some regions the Eskimos bend long willow branches into a series of arches to form a skeletal dome, then add layers of moss, dirt, and sod. For a window they use an animal skin with a peephole in it. If there's a bearded seal in the vicinity, his intestine will become the windowpane: Eskimos have found it to be not only weatherproof but also nearly transparent.

Air conditioning in this type of structure is crude but effective. A hole left in the sod and moss at top center serves as a smoke ventilator. An animal skin over the igloo entrance can be

Photos, Steve McCutcheon

With the encroachment of civilization —or at least its implements— snowmobiles and wood frame houses replace dogsleds and the traditional igloo. In some areas, this metamorphosis hangs half complete, and a home built with whalebone walls may be wired for electrical lighting.

partly or fully opened for fresh air intake, and a vent hole in the window can be closed by stuffing a whisk of hay through it.

The sod-wood-stone igloo often becomes a permanent home and receives such refinements as a stone fireplace under the smoke hole and raised stone or earthen beds covered with animal skins. Tanning and curing of these skins—not only for bedspreads but also for clothes, shoes, windows, doors, and tent walls —could be a problem. The Eskimos have a workable solution: their women simply chew the skins, hour after hour, until they are soft and flexible.

Nature and nurture

In each climatic region, the Eskimo takes the natural building products that are close at hand and improves them a little, but without interfering with their best natural properties. The melt-freeze treatment of snow blocks hard-

ens their crust for structural strength but does little to impair their insulating efficiency. Mama Eskimo's endless chewing on caribou hide and sealskin softens it but leaves it waterproof, not only for building but for clothing and boots. That it finally leaves her toothless is one of the penalties of Arctic life which fewer and fewer Eskimo women will be willing to pay.

HEOROT

Beowulf at home

Thirty men lie sleeping on hard wooden benches, in alcoves, and on the drafty floor of a great timbered hall: a combination fortress, castle, barracks, and rathskeller. Fires burn at two hearths, but the occupants—soldiers with shields and swords at their sides—are wrapped in animal skins against the chill northern night. There is a sudden crash. An enormous fist fells the split-log door with one blow, ripping it from its iron bolts and hinges. Every eye opens but the bodies are motionless, waiting, as a monstrous manlike creature, still dripping mudwater and trailing moss from the moors, advances on the prone warriors, his eyes burning. One man is seized and, as his comrades watch, frozen with terror, is devoured on the spot. The next man in the monster's path is not terrified: he has watched the

Seafarers at heart, Vikings in the time of Beowulf had already become consummate shipbuilders. When they turned their talents to building houses and halls, the same timbers turned up with the same joinery that held their boats together and, as seen here, even some of the same curving contours.

(Above) American Stock Photos from Tom Stack & Associates; (opposite page) Tom Stack & Associates

Historical Pictures Service, Chicago

attack and the gory feast as a study in fighting style, and he is ready when the intruder—Grendel—reaches for him and finds to his consternation that he has chosen the wrong victim. The great beast Grendel is suddenly in the grip of Beowulf, and he has eaten his last warrior.

The epic battle between Beowulf and Grendel has thrilled English-speaking people for a thousand years. It cost Grendel an arm, and the beast fled to die on the moors. It incited a retaliatory raid by Grendel's mother, a giant water hag who turned out to be even meaner than her son. To end *that* menace Beowulf had to fight mother alone in her cave, so deep under a lake that it took him an entire day of diving straight down to reach it. And somewhere, buried beneath layers of magic and marvel, lies the memory of a great mead hall where the first battle took place.

This was Heorot, site of the great English folk epic. It was not in England, but it did exist—in an age when real warriors fought real monsters (wolves, bears, and boars, if not fabulous beasts). They most certainly fought each other, and, in calmer times, they feasted and drank mead in real mead halls. Aside from Valhalla, and, assuming that Camelot was a castle rather than a hall, Heorot is the most renowned example of the mead halls that dotted England and northern Europe in premedieval times.

The fighters and feasters who inhabited these structures were the very early Vikings. Their way of building, like their way of life, was fairly crude, though often ingenious. Since their only architects were shipwrights, and since they had little use for stone ships, building design and construction centered around the working of wood and seldom strayed far from the configurations of boats: right-side-up at sea, upside-down on land. Norse builders erected wooden halls, houses, even castles, in places where stone was plentiful and timber scarce. So mead halls were timber and, like the American log cabin, were developed in Scandinavia and later exported.

The roots of *Beowulf*, like those of *Hamlet*, are in Denmark. Beowulf and his warriors were Geatas, whose home was southern Sweden early in the sixth century. They went to the aid of King Hrothgar at Heorot, probably on the island of Zealand off the Danish coast, and the story of their exploits was carried to England by Norse invaders who settled there in the seventh century. Handed down by word-of-mouth from one generation to the next, growing with each retelling, the legend was finally written down no earlier than the eighth century and possibly as late as the tenth, when the surviving manuscript was prepared by English monks.

By that time, the actual events that had inspired the poem had been magnified to mythic proportions. To begin a description of Heorot is to start with structural specifications screened through the beautiful but baffling overlays of poetry and lore as they appear in the poem itself:

To Hrothgar in time came triumph in battle,
The glory of the sword, and his friendly kinsmen
Flocked to serve him till the band of them was
   great,
A host of eager retainers. And his mind
Stirred him to command a hall to be built,
A huger mead-house[1] to be made and raised
Than any ever known to the children of men,
Where he under its roof to young and old
Would distribute such gifts as God gave him,
Everything but the lands and lives of his people.
Not few, we are told, were the tribes who then
Were summoned to the work far throughout this
   world,
To adorn that dwelling place. And so in due

time,
Quickly as men laboured, it was all prepared,
Most massive of halls; and he called it Heorot.
. . . The hall towered up
Clifflike, broad-gabled.[2] . . .

(Before Beowulf's arrival,)
He (Grendel) went then to visit at the full of night
That lofty hall, to see how the Danes
Fared as they lay at the end of their carousing.
Within it he found the band of warriors
Sleeping after the feast. . . .
. . . The creature was like a pestilence
   raging and ravenous, quick at his task,
Savage and unsparing, seizing thirty
Soldiers from their beds. . . .
Then it wasn't rare for a man elsewhere
At a greater distance to look for his rest,
For a bed in the outbuildings[3] . . . till empty
   and unvisited
Stood the best of halls.

(Beowulf's) . . . men hastened,
They marched together until they could see

1. Main functions of the mead house or hall were sleeping, eating, and carousing; and mead was the ever-flowing beverage: a fermented mix of honey, malt, water, and yeast.
2. Gables of Heorot were not only broad but high, and were adorned by stag antlers.
3. Outbuildings usually included cookhouse and storehouses, sometimes a buttery and a smithy, and separate sleeping quarters for women and children.
4. According to legend, Heorot's roof glinted with gold trim, reflecting flashes of sunlight visible far out to sea.
5. It's not clear whether the floors of Heorot were actually stone or wood. References to mead-benches being bolted to the floor seem to favor wood in a parquet "stone patterned" arrangement.

A timbered building resplendent with gold:
The most illustrious hall under heaven
For men to move in, and home of a king:
Like a lantern illuminating many lands.[4]
Here the soldier showed them the dazzling
Hall of the heroes. . . .

Grendel came stalking; he brought God's wrath.
His sin and violence thought to ensnare
One of our kind in that hall of halls.
He moved through the night till with perfect
     clearness
He could see the banquet-building, treasure-home
     of men
Gold panelled and glittering. . . .
. . . The door, firm iron-bound,
Flew at once ajar when he breached it with his
     fists:
The hall's mouth he tore wide open, enraged
And possessed by his evil. Quickly after this
The fiend stepped over the stone-patterned[5] floor.
(As Beowulf battled Grendel inside the hall:)
. . . Both hosts of the hall
Were in rage, in ferocity. The building

reverberated.
It was more than a marvel that that wine-house
Stood up to the battle-darers, that the splendid
     walls
Didn't fall to the ground; but it had the solidity.
It was cleverly compacted both inside and out
With its bands of iron.[6] Many were the mead-
     benches
Sumptuous with gold that were wrenched there
     from the floor,
Beside the antagonists in their epic fury.
—A thing undreamed of by Scylding wisdom
That any man could ever, in any manner,
Shatter it as it stood stately and horn-spanned[7]
By sleights disrupt it: till fire's[8] embrace
Should become its furnace.

(When the fight was over,)
Severely shattered was the shining building,
For all its inward iron-band-buttressing;
Its door hinges were sprung; only roof escaped
Without any damage when the slaughter-guilty
Deed-stained monster turned away in flight
Despairing of life.[9]

6. Viking timber structures used iron-band joinery,
a technique borrowed from their famed art of ship-
building. A buried Viking ship discovered at Sut-
ton Hoo on the southeastern English coast showed
remnants of these ironbound joints.
7. A reference to the fact that Heorot's roof was
adorned with stag horns. Heorot means *hart* or
stag.
8. Heorot was finally burned in the Danish Heatho-
bard vendetta.
9. *Beowulf* excerpts from verse translation by
Edwin Morgan originally published by The University of California Press; reprinted by permission of The Regents of the University of California.

Courtesy of the Royal Danish Ministry for Foreign Affairs

Historical Pictures Service, Chicago

When a story takes from two hundred to four hundred years to ripen before anyone writes it down, the details of its architecture are necessarily hazy. Archaeology can often help but, in this case, not a great deal. Thousands of graves have been excavated throughout Scandinavia and the Norse settlements in Britain. Many Viking ships have been raised and some reconstructed. But few buildings remain, and most of the survivors are houses: royal halls had a way of getting burned down after battles.

However, there are clues in the fascinating kinship between the longhouse or "fire hall"— the typical farm dwelling throughout the Viking age—and the other basic unit of Norse construction, the warship. One conjecture has it that primitive dwellings in northern European coastal regions often began with an overturned boat as a roof, supported on timber posts. Side walls of the early longhouses show a marked curvature—outward at the center and inward toward the gabled ends—in a boat shape that would mate with such a roof; there appears to be no other explanation for the curves. Whether or not an actual boat bottom ever topped a house, there is little question that home building in great seafaring cultures of the heroic age was dominated by Norse shipwrights whose talents for timberworking and joinery were the marvel of Europe.

Curiously, one point where these two trends most clearly converge is the remnant of Trelle-

120

Courtesy of the Royal Danish Ministry for Foreign Affairs

borg fortress, on the same island once occupied by Heorot and defended by Beowulf. Trelleborg guarded the west Zealand coast in the tenth century, at the height of Danish sea power under Cnut the Great, four centuries after the events of *Beowulf*. If a longhouse is reminiscent of an overturned Viking ship, this fortification can be seen as a capsized fleet. Its symmetrical layout enclosed sixteen garrison buildings arranged in four squares, all within a circular rampart, and fifteen slightly smaller houses outside. Curved sidewalls and straight end walls gave each house at least a crude resemblance to a truncated ship turned upside down, its ridgepole arched like a keel. It may have been more than coincidental that each

building (roughly a hundred feet long) had enough space to garrison one shipload of fighting men.

Like the smaller longhouse and the larger mead hall, the Trelleborg style of barracks building had a large stone hearth near the center, its fire vented through the roof, and raised sleeping platforms along each side wall. Apparently these barracks—and others defending headlands and key coastal regions throughout Scandinavia—were more Spartan versions of the great mead halls: more military and somewhat less festive, although it is true that excavation of grave sites in the Trelleborg camp has turned up the remains of a number of women.

Fighting was followed by feasting, distribution of spoils by the Chieftan —the ''ring-giver''—and the telling of tales about exploits in battle. The most stirring deeds (or the most eloquent claims) would be retold again and again and later sung by scops—roving Anglo Saxon minstrels. A few were finally written down and fewer still survive. Because an anonymous English monk now referred to as ''the Beowulf poet'' committed one such narrative song to writing, American school children now memorize passages of the great English epic about a Dane.

As to size, there is nothing left of Heorot to measure. From this point in history its proportions are no easier to assess than those of Camelot, which supposedly flourished in England at roughly the same time and has since undergone a similar escalation into legend.

Both, it may be assumed, were less ambitious in specifications than the great granddaddy of all mead halls, Valhalla, the home of Woden in Teutonic myth or Odin in the northlands. Valhalla had 540 doors, each wide enough to admit 800 soldiers abreast. Allowing three feet for each warrior with his shield, and assuming that walls occupied three times the width of doors, Woden's mead hall was 5,184,000 feet in circumference, roughly the size of Pennsylvania!

One might expect Valhalla, like Heorot, to be a timber structure, since in the traditions of Teutonic myth and Norse poetry the universe was supported by a gigantic tree. But in fact Woden's hall was described as having a framework of spears and a roof of shields, form following function to the extent that Valhalla was the place where fallen warriors were sent after death, fully equipped with spears and shields.

In Iceland, where neither spears nor timbers were plentiful, Norsemen overcame their predilection for timber in boatbuilding configurations and instead erected stone walls and turf roofing. Viking settlers in the Orkneys and Shetlands used alternating layers of stone and earth or turf. Norwegians under Eirik, or Erik, left remnants of similar structures in Greenland. Had they left the same traces in "Vinland," they might have prevented a good deal of argument over who discovered America.

THE TROUBLE WITH CABINS AND COTTAGES

**Early American alternatives
to the log cabin and the White House**

The great houses of early America and the architectural influences they embody have been widely noted, thoroughly documented, and often restored or replicated. Humbler dwellings, quite properly, have received less frequent and less lavish attention. Not so properly, the cabins and cottages in which the overwhelming majority of early Americans were raised have been somewhat garbled in popular histories. We can, however, explore a few of the curious twists through which the American cabin and cottage have come.

American Stock Photos from Tom Stack and Associates

In the early 1840s, with the help of William Henry Harrison's "log cabin and hard cider" campaign, the log cabin clinched its place as a symbol of America and all but dislodged other early dwellings from the national memory. (A superb documentation of how this happened may be found in *The Log Cabin Myth* by Harold Shurtleff, introduced and edited by Samuel Eliot Morison and published by Harvard University Press in 1939.)

Architects, however, were not leaving modest dwellings and humble origins entirely to the politicians. While Harrison and Tyler stumped the country, visiting the party faithful in hastily built log-cabin headquarters, horticulturist and "rural architect" Andrew Jackson Downing was working on a book to be called *Cottage Residences*. And architect John Bul-

lock, editor of a textbook series on the rudiments of architecture, was planning to publish *The American Cottage Builder*. Both books appeared between the two great log-cabin campaigns: those of Harrison and Lincoln.

As for the log cabin as an architectural genre, it is roughly as American as apple pie, which was invented by the Romans. The familiar sight of a crude but sturdy dwelling of round logs— notched, crossed at the ends, protruding at each corner, chinked with clay, and topped by a roof of split oak shingles—was not at all a familiar sight to the first settlers who colonized this country, a century of grade-school history textbooks notwithstanding.

Jamestown was settled by English small-town and country folk in 1607. Back home James I was feuding with the House of Commons over

Historical Pictures Service, Chicago

union with Scotland. Oliver Cromwell was flunking arithmetic at the Huntingdon free school. Scholars at Oxford were shaking their heads over odd new theories from someone named Kepler in Germany and Galileo Galilei in Italy. Londoners were still buzzing about William Shakespeare's new play, *Antony and Cleopatra*. But the countryside was just as the emigrants had left it: the houses were framed with timbers and walled with clapboard or wattle and daub, and those were the only houses that the colonists knew how to build, or would want to build.

At first they erected temporary shelters, notably wigwams, which they also knew how to build because the basic bentwood construction technique was similar to that of the English garden arbor. But soon the sawyers and car-penters were at work, riving clapboard; hewing timbers for joists, studs, corner posts, and rafters; and neatly mortising corner joints for perma-nent frame houses. It would be thirty-one years before an English colonist would see his first log cabin, and a good deal longer before any of them would see fit to build one.

When the log cabin did arrive, it came from Sweden. Apparently it was the Scandinavians who invented the architectural link to Lincoln; but by the seventeenth century log cabins were common in northern Europe from Norway to the Volga. Even earlier roots have been found in Stone-Age European lake villages, where some houses used crossed logs, overlapping at the corners. But it was not until 1638 that the round-log house reached the Western Hemisphere; more precisely, it reached Dela-

127

By 1700, the log cabin was a favorite first home for frontiersmen who had the Northern European knack of notching logs for tight fits and plumb corners (below). Colonists with different backgrounds might favor stone, thatch, mud brick, or stucco construction. Among Nevada's earliest settlers (right) two new neighbors used what skills they brought with them to build different sorts of shelter.

Barry Hennings from Photo Researchers

Barry Hennings from Photo Researchers

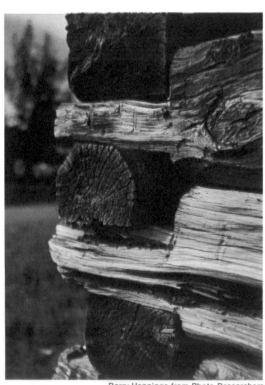

Barry Hennings from Photo Researchers

ware Bay with the founding of New Sweden, roughly midway in time between Columbus and Lincoln.

Log-house construction spread, but slowly and not in all directions. The English and Dutch ignored it. New England and Virginia continued to build English medieval cottages, with more elaborate English manor houses for the affluent. In Philadelphia brick walls went up over timber framing. But German and Scotch-Irish frontiersmen were carrying the log cabin west. In the wilderness, the land could be cleared as the log house was built—sturdy, cozy, defensible, fast, and without the need of precious "nayles."

The true log cabin was normally a temporary wilderness shelter, serving the frontier family until there was time to build a larger, better-appointed house out of hewn logs, mortised at the corners, with a wood floor, iron hinges, a stone chimney, and glass windows. The first cabin was likely to have a dirt floor, leather hinges, a wooden chimney (if any) with clay lining, and greased paper or skins for window coverings. Roof shingles were split oak, ash, or cedar, held in place by weight poles. The cabin could literally be built with no nails or hardware, and with no tool other than an axe—but it wasn't easy. Unless good, regular pine or spruce logs were available, huge gaps between logs had to be chinked with chips, sticks, straw, moss, clay, mud, or some combination of these. Notching the logs for a tight fit and plumb corners was a special skill that the early settlers, except for the Swedes, simply did not have.

Proliferation of log cabins began in earnest around 1700 and soon predominated in most new frontier settlements. After the Revolution, a new nation was ready to romanticize its dra-

Made of good, even logs of spruce or pine, mortised at the corners (left), a sturdy cabin could be built without the need of scarce, expensive, sometimes unobtainable nails. Between logs, chinking with clay and other filler (far left) closed up any gaps and helped to insulate. When extra fastening was needed (below), the builder could always resort to wooden pegs or wooden nails.

matic wilderness origins. Since publicity was still a fledgling art, it took a little time; but in 1840, when a Democratic newspaper sniffed that William Henry Harrison would be better suited to a log cabin than to the White House, the Whigs seized on the slur and turned it into the famed "log cabin and hard cider" imagery of The "Tippecanoe and Tyler too" campaign.

That campaign launched the legend that the lore of Abraham Lincoln would climax twenty years later. Two centuries of architectural history came unstuck, and before long every schoolboy could tell the story of the Pilgrim wading ashore, axe in hand, and inventing log-cabin technology on the spot. Older boys — scholars, historians, politicians, illustrators, and the planners of centennials — filled books, speeches, articles, and pageants with the same myths well into the twentieth century.

During the hubbub of the Harrison cam-

paign men like Downing and Bullock shared the country's preoccupation with humble dwellings, but not with nostalgia. Their eyes were on private visions of a future in which they saw attractive homes for the poor as well as the rich. For the rich Downing had designed landscaping and gardens along the Hudson, and he had planned the grounds for the Capitol, the White House, and the Smithsonian. Now he designed — and Bullock compiled the designs of others — for everyone, with cottages that started at $200.

From this distance a few charming and perfectly practical cottage plans appear to be buried in a gallery that ranges from the curious to the downright eccentric. But in looking at a few of the designs from *The American Cottage Builder*, it is well to remember that most of these plans had already been built, in one nonplussed neighborhood or another.

129

A century before Henry Ford set out to make the $300 automobile, architect John Bullock was figuring out the $300 house. In *The American Cottage Builder*, he included the Model cottage developed by Prince Albert for improvement of England's poor but favored more basic designs such as the Thatched cottage.

The model cottage

"I hope the day is far distant when Prince Albert's Model Cottages will be thought an appropriate residence for an American laborer. The room is too confined, the size is too small for our people." With this scolding, Bullock presents the model cottage erected by Queen Victoria's consort for the great Crystal Palace exhibition of 1851. Planned for four families, the structure enclosed a living room, bedroom, and pantry for each. Albert, always alert for ways to apply science to the improvement of society, used the models to promote hollow bricks for insulation, cast-iron springers, and wrought iron tie-rods.

Thatched cottage

"Very suitable for lodges," the thatched cottage is offered as an apt blend with the scenery of the country. "Straw thatching," Bullock points out, "is a covering easily provided in any agricultural vicinity, and is capable of being repaired from time to time at trifling cost: but it is easily accessible to vermin, and, therefore, objectionable, for the better class of cottages." Instead, he recommends reed, to be woven by experienced thatchers, with creeping plants spread over the surface of the roof. All told: a living room, kitchen, two bedrooms, veranda, tool house, and outbuildings for $400 to $900. Columns are unbarked oak; occasionally upper branches were left on two adjacent columns to form an arch.

Bullock's designs ranged from Rural Home No. 1 (floor plan below), intended for an orchard setting, to duplex tenant cottages for the poor.

Rural home no. 1

Attributed to Swiss influence, this cottage is suggested for rural or suburban settings along the Hudson, where Downing had designed and landscaped many homes. Ideally, the author says, it will be surrounded by greenery and orchards, with "the luscious peach, with its downy cheek, the buttery, melting pear, the red-cheeked cherry, the golden apricot; and, peeping out, nearly smothered by its own habiliments, the never-cloying delicacy of the strawberry, as if to escape that inevitable destiny peculiar to strawberries, of being smothered in cream." The cottage? "Perfectly simple in form—the variety in the external elevation being produced by the projecting roof." Estimated cost: $1,300.

Cottage of the Society for Improving the Condition of the Poor

For an estimated $800 to $1000, this duplex would provide each occupant a living room "fourteen-six by fifteen feet . . . thus affording the utmost possible space for the little furniture which the tenant may have to arrange in his 'best room.'" A scullery and pantry are attached in the back, which is actually the front since it also includes the entrances and a three-foot-square lobby for each. "The aid of the cottager would of course be expected," the architect notes, "to train honeysuckle or whatever he most desires along its frontage."

Gothic suburban cottage

Listed as the residence of C. Prescott, Esq., Troy, New York, this house was designed, Downing is led to believe, "by his intelligent lady, Mrs. Prescott, who, not being an architect, called to her aid H. Thayer, the Architect by whose united labors the designs and plans were completed." Apparently uncertain whether the word "cottage" quite suits an eighteen-room, $15,000 residence, Downing elsewhere calls it a "villa."

The village cottage

This design is described as "much recommended and adopted in England" and as "suitable for mechanics." Stone walls are eighteen inches thick. The first floor consists entirely of a 15- by 13-foot living room, a 19- by 13-foot kitchen, and a small pantry beneath the stairs to the bedrooms above. Out of sight in back is a lean-to building against the kitchen, "divided into a washhouse or scullery and fitted up with the usual conveniences, and a tool house and the requisite out-offices."

Stretching the word ''cottage'' a bit, Downing presented an 18-room Gothic manor house. Less expensive models included the Village Cottage for workers, an octagonal house (floor plan below), and an Italian Cottage recommended for commanding sites.

Suburban octagonal cottage

William H. Wilcox designed this octagonal house and urged its advantages over rectangular and ''irregular'' plans: ''The octangular cottage encloses one-fifth more superficial area (with a given extent of external wall) than the square,'' Wilcox wrote. ''It offers less resistance to the wind, looks equally well from all points of view, and furnishes an abundant supply of closets. It can be built well (if of wood) for about $1,500.''

Italian cottages

Not to be wasted in valley or town, the Italian cottage is suggested for ''a position visible from a considerable distance, and commanding from its site an extensive view.'' The tower is ''eight feet and a half high,'' to be used as a porch on the ground floor and a bedroom upstairs. Estimated cost of the cottage: $400 to $900 in 1850 currency.

Plain and fancy. While some Easterners opted for stylizations such as the Byzantine Cottage (which Bullock included but frowned on), Southwesterners were finding the Prairie Cottage (floor plan below) as adaptable to their frontier as was the log cabin in more heavily wooded territories.

Byzantine cottage

In a neat piece of circular reasoning, Bullock dismisses the Byzantine cottage and omits further description: "The Byzantine Cottage does not ordinarily suit the general observer," he reports. "The reason is, because it is Byzantine, and is in this country out of place." He does include a cost estimate: $2,500.

Prairie cottage

The direct competitor of the log cabin at the time Downing and Bullock were writing was this frontier cottage of unburnt brick: "peculiarly adapted to settlers in the Western States." (For an unburnt brick recipe, see the next page.) Planned size is 28 by 18 feet, to include a 16-foot-square kitchen-washroom-pantry-living room and two small bedrooms on the first floor. Outer walls rise three or four feet above the joists to make a loft large enough for "a lodging room over the bedroom, or it may accommodate boarders."

Where logs were scarce, bricks could be made of ordinary clay and straw. Lacking a kiln, the settler could sun-dry his bricks and be ready to start construction in ten or twelve days.

How to make unburnt brick

Henry Leavitt Ellsworth (Yale, class of 1810) was a lawyer, U.S. commissioner of patents, and close friend of Washington Irving. He was also the author of a publication entitled *Plan for Cheap Cottages*, in which he instructs the frontier farmer or rancher on making bricks for a house such as the Prairie Cottage shown here:

Select a suitable spot of ground, as near the place of building as practicable, and let a circle, ten feet or more be described; let the loam be removed and the clay dug up one foot thick; or, if the clay is not found on the spot, let it be carted in to that depth. Any ordinary clay will answer. Tread this clay with cattle, and add some straw cut six or eight inches long—using two common bundles to one hundred brick. After the clay is tempered by working it, the material is duly prepared for the brick. A mould is then formed of plank, of the size of the brick desired.

In England, they are usually made eighteen inches long, one foot wide, and nine inches thick. I have found the most convenient size to be one foot long, six inches wide, and six inches thick. The mould should have a bottom not air-tight, since mortar will not fall when a vacuum is produced. The clay is then spread in the moulds in the same manner that brick moulds are ordinarily filled. A wire or piece of iron hoop will answer very well for striking off the top. One man will mould about as fast as another man can carry away—two moulds being used by him. The bricks are placed upon the level ground where they are suffered to dry for two days, turning them edgewise the second day; and then packed in a pile, protected from the rain, and left ten or twelve days to dry.

For mortar Ellsworth recommends three parts clay, two parts ashes, and one part sand—also usable for plaster if lime is not available for lime plaster.

135

THE FIRST HOUSES

Neolithic notes on urban planning

In attempting to connect the past with the present, some explorers work against tighter deadlines than others. The paleontologist can rummage for specimens safely preserved in tar or fossilized in rock for thirty million years. The archaeologist knows that if his grant doesn't come through this spring, a town or tomb buried for five thousand years can probably wait one more.

The cultural anthropologist, on the other hand, has to get there while the poles are still wet, the fish are still frying, and someone is ready to tell stories after supper and exhibit some "behavior," all before the arrival of the highway department or the transistor radio. Doomed to lose many such races, scholars in the field of "urgent anthropology" rush to catalog primitive cultures before they are modernized beyond recognition. Unrecorded language, customs, traditions, and folklore can simply evaporate.

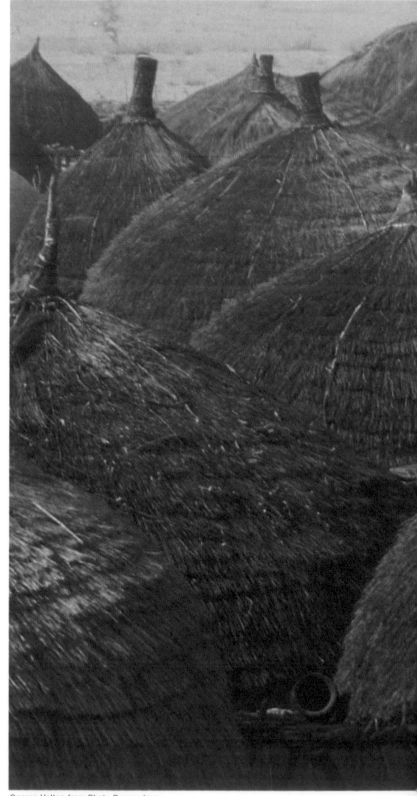

George Holton from Photo Researchers

In a Hausa village grass thatched roofs are supported by low walls or stilted frames. The roof is sometimes fashioned on the ground and lifted into place. If the walls or frame rot, the roof can be easily transported to a new location.

Malcolm Kirk from Peter Arnold

(Right) From the air, this orderly arrangement could almost pass for a suburban subdivision dotted with swimming pools. On the ground, it is a rudimentary village in Chad, whose economy is almost entirely based on farming and cattle raising. Some primitive buildings, such as this Abelam house (above) in New Guinea are decorated in an ages-old style that would elicit the envy of pop culture artists.

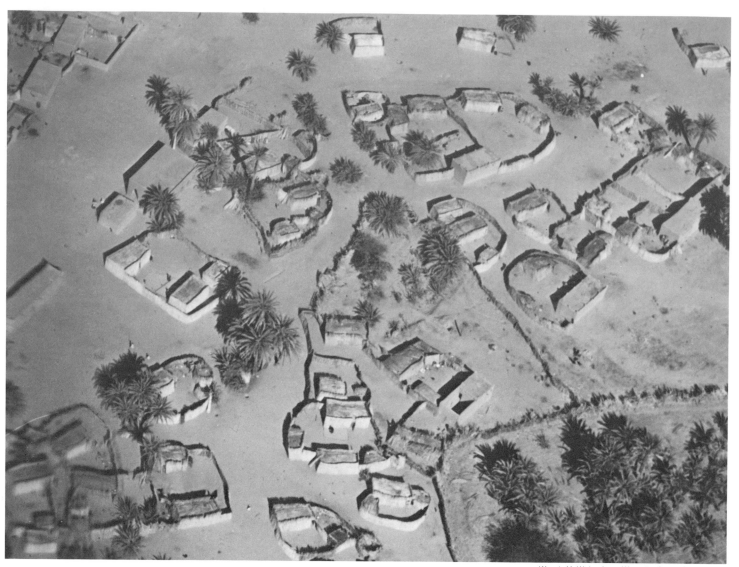

Wendy V. Weiss from Woodfin Camp & Associates

Dwellings are more durable, but as the least monumental of architecture they are the most vulnerable to extinction. The marvelous thing about primitive houses—unless you live in one—is that although they don't last long, they do persist. Most of the kinds of shelter built before and throughout history are still being built—in some fashion, in some region. And where houses are clustered in villages, towns, and cities, most of the municipal problems of Jericho or Carthage will eventually turn up in Muncie.

Urban Renewal

Neolithic land villages in Europe, and later in Africa, practiced their own devastating brand of slum clearance and renewal. At frequent intervals, they simply burned the hut—or the entire village—to the ground, routing the accumulated vermin and eliminating the problem of rot in their wood poles and thatching. Dislocation of families was not a problem: most of the buildings were small one- and two-room huts that could be reconstructed in a few hours.

138

A beehive dwelling in Niger blends naturally into the surroundings from which its building materials were taken virtually unchanged. Stilts raise the house above ground, protecting its inhabitants from groundwater and from wild animals.

Conical thatched grass roofs top circular dwellings built with interlaced fiber siding in a mountain village in New Guinea (right). In New Herbides (below) bamboo poles and palm leaves provide the building materials.

Jack Fields from Photo Researchers

Kal Muller from Woodfin Camp & Associates

Building Codes

The Yagua tribe of Peru uses plaited palm leaves for roof and walls, over a lashed-pole frame. Throughout the tropics, vines and the veins of palm fronds have been used as lashing straps for thousands of years. Favorite plaster base: clay or puddled anthill earth.

Thatched grass, leaves, or reed matting form conical or gabled roofs in many parts of Africa and South America. Some Polynesian dwellings have interlaced coconut-fiber siding. Among American Indians, birch bark was favored not only for canoes but for wall and roof coverings, wall linings, and even for carpeting. Tropical tree bark often serves as shingles in African forest regions, but thatching is more common because, properly plaited, it is nearly waterproof. (A compromise from Sumatra: In one tribe men use thatching on the roof, and women wear the bark.)

In Arctic and tundra regions of northern Europe, remnants have been found of huts built by stretching skins over frames of large whale and walrus bones. And an Australian folktale describes a house built of emu and kangaroo

140

George Holton from Photo Researchers

Thatched grass or leaves form conical or gabled roofs in many parts of Africa (left) and South America (bottom). Once the roof is complete, the same material may find its way into ceremonial costume design.

bones and covered with animal hides—quite possibly kangaroo hides.

The Sakai of Malaysia still build some of their houses in trees. In the absence of lifts and cranes, building materials must be light enough to climb with. Flooring consists of bamboo bound with rattan. Walls are rattan, and the roof is made of attap leaves, which have a life expectancy of from four to ten years. Since the attap grows leaves up to ten feet long and four feet wide, one leaf sometimes does the entire roofing job.

Carl Frank from Photo Researchers

141

One culture erects golden arches over its hamburger stands; another adorns its granaries to draw good luck or friendly spirits to the harvest. Giant, smiling faces were carved or painted on the sides of old African granaries to invite good fortune. Newer models are more matter-of-fact, but an intricately carved door in Mali (bottom) invokes benign providence at the entry to a Dogon storage bin.

Facades

Since prehistoric times, food storehouses have been invested (and sometimes adorned) with personalities whose moods signify prosperity or famine. Legend has it that the stilted granaries of the ancient Iberians used to come to life and dance in the night. Some of their anthropomorphic cousins in Africa are still smiling.

Loren A. McIntyre from Woodfin Camp & Associates

Master Plan: Transportation, Refuse Disposal, and Food Supplies

Few planners would care to lump these categories together, but consider the *de facto* master plan of pole-hut villages built over water. These began in the Late Stone Age and still exist in the marshes of Cambodia and New Guinea and the inner reaches of the Amazon. Transportation is by water. Garbage disposal is into water. And a good part of the food supply comes out of the water. Nor do residents have far to paddle for hunting and fishing: the refuse they throw into the water attracts marsh fowl and fish to the village.

Marc & Evelyne Bernheim from Woodfin Camp & Associates

143

Photos, David Muench

Sheltered by the sandstone cliffs of Colorado, Mesa Verde survives the elements to stand as a well-preserved remnant of a civilization that flourished a thousand years ago. The history of some of the pueblo people is recorded in petroglyphs carved into the cliffs.

Condominiums

Within a country which thinks of itself as beginning its third century are pueblo Indian tribes (including the Pueblo tribe itself) whose people have been cultivating crops for forty centuries and building towns for fifteen. Their settlements first honeycombed the Southwestern hillsides with subterranean apartments, then gradually evolved the communal architecture of the pueblos. Examples of both survive in the tableland of Mesa Verde in southwest Colorado (now a national park), showing development of clay and stone pueblo clusters by 800 AD.

None of this was "discovered" until a hundred years ago. The first small cliff houses were noted in a survey taken in the 1870s, and in 1888 two startled cattlemen found "Cliff Palace," a multistoried complex of more than 200 rectangular apartments and circular ceremonial chambers.

In the meantime, the U. S. Bureau of Ethnology had responded to the first discoveries with an 1885 expedition sent to explore ancient dwellings of the Supai and Santa Clara Indians. After digging into a series of caves carved out of volcanic rock, the group glumly reported evidence "piled two and three feet thick" that the caves were stables, not dwellings.

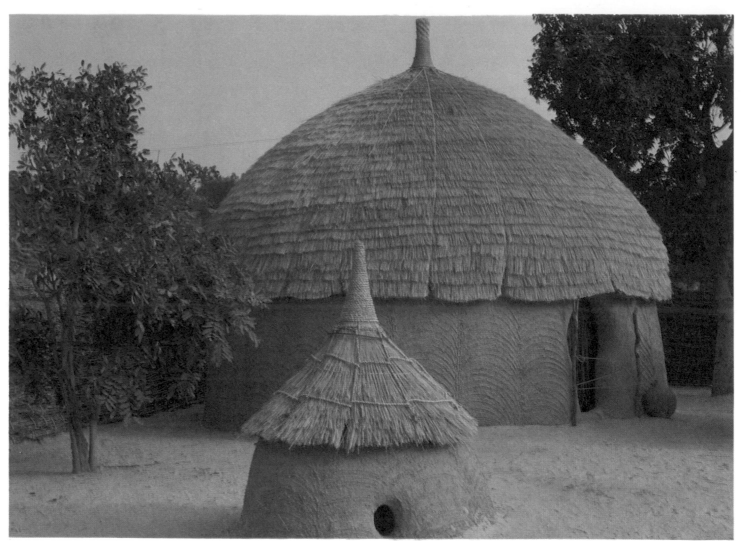

Diane Rawson from Photo Researchers

Multifamily Dwellings

Remains have been found of Stone-Age villages with houses large enough for five to twenty families. Sometimes there were separate dwellings for women and children and large dormitories for men, an arrangement that persists in some parts of Africa, Borneo, and Melanesia. In the highly developed lake villages of the Bronze Age, rectangular pile dwellings often covered an area of 80 to 100 square yards. Space was divided into a large, open platform and various rooms, including a kitchen and workroom and a living and sleeping area with a fireplace, beds, and often a loom.

Zoning Variances

Where polygamy is practiced, distinctions between single-family and multifamily dwellings tend to blur. In one version of the African *kraal* there is a separate hut for each wife and her children, enclosed in a palisade along with the master's house, to which the favorite wife has access and other wives are occasionally invited.

Population Shifts

Each nomadic culture develops its own brand of portable shelter. The Bedouin tent consists of a ridgepole supported by sticks and covered with a cloth made of goat hair. The "tipi" or "tepee," used by the Dakota, Cree, Chippewa, and others, served as both shelter and luggage. For travel, the Indians wrapped their utensils, tools, and weapons in the tipi cover and often dragged it from place to place using the tent poles as a skid. Perhaps the simplest of all temporary shelters is the "benab,"

an instant hut made by roving hunters in Guyana. They lay a few palm leaves out flat, bind their stalks together, and stick them in the ground. The leaves form an arched shelter roof.

Semang pygmies of the Malay Peninsula and a related tribe on the Andaman Islands in the Bay of Bengal have another version of the portable hut. They simply prop up a plaited mat and sleep to leeward. In more permanent camps, this mat is raised on four posts to form a slanted roof, or two mats are joined in a saddle roof. The Andamanese place these huts in a rough circle around a cleared dancing ground.

Dan Budnik from Woodfin Camp & Associates

147

Nomadic herdsmen cross the Sahara (right) and the steppes of Central Mongolia (bottom left) seeking new pastures for their livestock. On reaching his destination, the Mongolian nomad will erect a yurt (bottom right), a cone-shaped tent made of overlapping felt mats. In Niger the portable dwelling (below) consists of mats or animal hides supported on curved poles.

Photos, George Holton from Photo Researchers

Wendy V. Watriss from Woodfin Camp & Associates.

Moving day—don't forget to bring the house. Personal belongings of the Fulani nomads are limited to bare necessities. This and the spare design of his shelter enable the tribesman to travel light. The dwelling is simply dismantled and carried along with personal possessions on the back of a long-horned steer.

Photos, Victor Englebert from Photo Researchers

149

Certain pitfalls to avoid
in building
a fifteen-million-dollar house

FOUQUET'S FOLLY

Nothing was too good for Nicolas Fouquet. As the second most powerful man in France, he required a country estate suitable to his station. As a man of superlative taste and a patron of the arts, he was able to assemble for the task the most gifted architects, artists, sculptors, and craftsmen of seventeenth-century France. And as a nimble superintendent of finance under Louis XIV, he had his construction budget wired to the national treasury.

Marie-Claire from Paris-Match

Vaux-le-Vicomte: pride of Nicolas Fouquet, envy of Louis XIV, inspiration for the palace at Versailles—and quite possibly the grandest *faux pas* in the history of the French court.

The result was Vaux-le-Vicomte, 50 kilometers southeast of Paris, a magnificent château whose planning was so perfect that history recalls only one flaw: it was better than the king's.

Louis XIV was twenty-three years old. His activities to that time had been largely concerned with horses, hunting, and girls, while the running of France had been left to the young king's preceptor and chief minister, Mazarin.

When Mazarin died in March of 1661, it was Nicolas Fouquet who inherited much of his power and had every expectation of acquiring it all. Born of the lesser nobility, Fouquet had risen to the titles of Viscount of Melun and of Vaux, Minister of State, Superintendent of Finance, and Procurer General.

He was renowned as a financial wizard, a wealthy man by virtue of two matrimonial masterpieces, and the most surefooted traveler through the labyrinth of loyalties and venalities that characterized the French Court.

Fouquet's stature can be measured by his guest list. His party in the summer of 1661 to exhibit the new château at Vaux was attended by the entire Court, including the king, who had to don layer upon layer of ruffles and lace and endure a three-hour carriage ride from Fontainebleau under an August sun.

Jean Roubier

Louis was soon to forget the heat. What he encountered at Vaux-le-Vicomte was enough to recall more substantial annoyances—enough to make a man grow suddenly tired of living at the Louvre and summering at Fontainebleau, and enough to make an ambitious young king wonder if the royal treasury was any longer big enough for two.

For the building of Vaux, Louis and the taxpayers of France had unwittingly furnished at least a million *livres*, at least fifteen million dollars in today's currency. Not that Fouquet was doing anything unusual; other finance ministers had siphoned before him. But none of his predecessors had made such a spectacular display of their profits.

The King's entourage approached the château through a vast forecourt laced with broad avenues, manicured groves and hedges, outbuildings faced with matching stone, finally a moat and, just beyond it, the house itself: a massive structure designed for Fouquet by Louis Le Vau, who was later to serve as architect for the palace at Versailles.

Huge, ornate, bristling with mansards (Mansard himself was still alive), embellished with statuary, and crowned by a sixty-foot dome, Vaux mated French château traditions with a

153

Andre Le Notre, designer of the Tuileries, devised an ingenious system of perspective for the vast gardens of Vaux. Transverse axes of water connecting the garden's 250 fountains create an optical illusion that makes the chateau seem nearer.

strong Italian influence. Inside, the design genius of Le Vau blended with the artistic genius of Charles Le Brun, who had drained the reservoirs of French talent to assemble a task force of nine hundred artists, sculptors, and craftsmen for the interior-decoration project. In nearby Maincy he had built an entire furniture and textile factory, specializing in tapestries, just to supply the walls and halls of Vaux-le-Vicomte.

Louis toured the grand salon under the dome, a cluster of huge tributary rooms around it, and a series of apartments—any one of which would have put the king's own quarters to shame. Friezes, tapestries, endless sculpture and relief, decorative fixtures and molding were just the beginning. The walls and ceilings were alive with epic after epic in mural and fresco—several acres of allegory and symbolism—climaxed by Hercules on Olympus. It wasn't entirely clear whether Hercules was meant to symbolize the king or Fouquet.

Like too much candy, the beauty might have become unbearable; but Louis got no relief when he stepped out onto a balustraded walkway overlooking the gardens. More magnificence. André Le Nôtre, designer of the Tuileries, had now designed the gardens of Vaux. Peopled with statuary in marble and gilded lead, the gardens boasted at least fifty major fountains and scores of sparkling jets and sprays.

Fountains and waterways were placed by Le Nôtre according to a private geometry that defied ordinary perspective. For example, he used transverse axes of water to reflect sunlight in such a way that a visitor walking out into the gardens had the illusion that—although the foreground kept receding as he moved away from the house—the house itself seemed to remain near. But from where the king stood, the scale alone was overwhelming. Beyond moats, groves, grottoes, terraces, and cascades,

154

he could see a towering statue of Hercules, the crown jewel of the gardens. Hercules was two miles away.

If the architecture and ornamentation of Vaux were overdone (the king through so), house-warming festivities supplied the *coup de grâce*. Their cultural equivalent today would have to include a serenade by Leonard Bernstein, commemorative verse by Robert Lowell, theatricals by Stanley Kubrick and Neil Simon, catering by Lutece, and a massed salute by the Seventh Fleet.

For Fouquet it was dinner by Vatel, the finest chef in France, served to music composed and conducted by the country's most prominent musician, Lully. Then a new play written by (and starring) Molière, poetry by La Fontaine and Pellisson; and finally an apocalyptic display of fireworks by Torelli of Italy, climaxed by exploding *fleurs-de-lis* and Roman candles from the rooftop, to the accompaniment of trumpet and cannon.

Three weeks later Fouquet was arrested by the musketeer D'Artagnan (later celebrated by Alexandre Dumas, but for other feats). The charge was embezzlement, and the warrant was signed by the king. If Fouquet's detractors in the Royal Court had not been able to convince Louis that the treasury was bleeding, Vaux *had* convinced him. Then too, the young monarch had something else on his mind: Versailles.

Before poor Fouquet was even convicted, Louis was having shrubbery and statuary

Marie-Claire from Paris-Match

On leaving Vaux, the King sent Fouquet's geniuses (and his furnishings) to Versailles—to do the same thing, only bigger.

hauled from Vaux to the site of his own great construction project.

Dazzled by Vaux, Louis had decided to dazzle the rest of Europe. Before he was through, nearly every feature of Vaux had been incorporated in the new palace at Versailles, only bigger.

Louis expropriated not only the ornaments of Vaux but its geniuses as well. Le Vau was his architect; Le Brun designed his interiors; and Le Nôtre laid out his gardens. Virtually the entire community of artisans working at Maincy moved to Versailles. And when the new palace was ready for its first feasting, Molière was there with a play, Vatel with a dinner, La Fontaine with a poem, Lully with a recital, and—sure enough—Torelli with his fireworks.

As for Fouquet, he had too many admirers to be executed as Louis had intended. He was imprisoned for sixteen years, dying just before he was to be set free. And Vaux-le-Vicomte, after many generations and two restorations, stands today very much as it was in 1661.

Its preservation is fortunate: there will never be another like it. Today's architect cannot monopolize a nation's artists and craftsmen, as Le Vau and Le Brun could. Nor can he build an on-site tapestry factory, nor arrange the topless budget that Fouquet enjoyed with his direct, unmetered pipeline from the treasury. For that matter, where would an architect in this century find a client willing to foot the water bill for Le Nôtre's 250 fountains?

157

CONFUSION AROUND THE GLOBE

In April of 1597 the lease ran out on a small piece of land in the Shoreditch section of London. The landlord, one Giles Allen, refused to renew on the grounds that his tenants' activities had been boisterous, unruly, and vulgar. Some historians think Allen had a more compelling reason: with the tenants evicted, he stood to acquire their building — a large wooden theater called The Theatre.

The name was not as unimaginative as it may sound. When it opened in 1576, The Theatre had indeed been *the* theater in London and perhaps the first public playhouse in English history. The builder — Allen's tenant — was James Burbage, an actor in the days when players had to perform as best they could in the inn yards along Gracious (now Gracechurch) street.

The cloud-capp'd towers, the gorgeous
    palaces,
The solemn temples, the great globe itself,
Yea, all which it inherit, shall dissolve
And, like this insubstantial pageant faded,
Leave not a rack behind. We are such stuff
As dreams are made on. . . .

The Tempest. Act IV. Scene 1

Three hundred years before photography, London's illustrators had too many buildings to keep track of, except sketchily. Thus historians have had to sort through such versions of the Globe as these: (clockwise from top left) a 1599 Woodcut, published later in London's *Penny Magazine*; a 1616 drawing from Visscher's View of London; a section of the 1638 rendering of the city's Bankside district, by Merian; and an eighteenth century drawing probably based on an earlier work like Merian's.

Famed Elizabethan clown Richard Tarleton (below) annoyed Shakespeare by injecting his own lines into the plays. The Bard retaliated in the person of Hamlet. After deciding "The play's the thing/ Wherein I'll catch the conscience of the king," Hamlet instructs the actors: ". . . Let those that play your clowns speak no more than is set down for them. That's villainous, and shows a most pitiful ambition in the fool that uses it."

Once Burbage had set the example, the great wooden "plaie howses" of London proliferated: the Swan, the Rose, the Fortune, the Hope, and the Curtain. Each housed an accomplished repertory company with its own playwrights, plus at least one quick-penned copyist to pirate plays from the other theaters. The actors would perform in their playhouse during fall, winter, and spring, then go on summer tour in the country when hot weather and city crowds aggravated the plague.

With his competitors flourishing and his lease about to expire, Burbage built a new and even finer theater on the west side of London, converting a building once used by the monks of Blackfriars into England's first roofed-in, lighted public theater. But Blackfriars was in an exclusive residential enclave whose occupants did not care for the idea of drums, cannon, trumpets, and the "vagrant and lewd persons" that

the performance of plays might attract. They petitioned the Privy Council and tried to have Blackfriars suppressed.

Burbage died less than two months later. His sons, Richard and Cuthbert, reacted differently. They contacted several friends, including a builder named Peter Street and a young actor and playwright named William Shakespeare. With Blackfriars in trouble and The Theatre in the hands of the landlord, the Burbages formed a syndicate and attempted to negotiate an extension of the lease. When that failed, they took matters into their own hands.

Three days after Christmas of 1598 the Burbages, Shakespeare, four other actors, and some hired help arrived in Shoreditch with wrecking bars and, under Street's expert direction, commenced to dismantle The Theatre and cart off its timbers across the Thames to Bankside. (Allen later claimed that, in addition to

Convent garden

S. Clement

Somerset h.   Arundel house

Essex house   Temple stayres   Temple

Blackfreyars

The Globe

Beere bayting h.

By permission of the Folger Shakespeare Library, Washington, D.C.

The cartographers who pictured London when the Globe still stood have confounded latter day scholars with radically different notions of the theater's shape, size, and placement. In *Hollar's View of London, 1647*, the Globe is mislabeled "Beere Bayting," the real Bear Garden is marked, "The Globe," and the theater is shown as circular instead of octangular. In Hollar's defense, it should be remembered that he was attempting an aerial view before there were airplanes.

wrecking bars, the company also brandished swords, daggers, and axes and behaved in a "very riotous, outrageous, and forcible manner." He sued for damages and lost.)

On Bankside, in a section called the Liberty of Clink in Southwark, the syndicate used its salvaged timbers to erect the finest playhouse in London and the premiere house for most of Shakespeare's plays: the Globe.

Few structures have ever received the scholarly attention that has been lavished on the Globe. Careers have been poured into the minutiae of circumstantial evidence that hints at its size, shape, construction, interior, stage design, and the relationship of these to Elizabethan theatrical technique. There are many sources of indirect evidence, including inferences drawn from the stage directions in

Popular characters of Shakespeare's day appear on a candlelit stage (top) in a seventeenth century woodcut. Included is Falstaff who was introduced on the Globe Theater stage in 1597 in Part One of *Henry IV*. (Bottom) Macbeth and Banquo encounter the three Weird Sisters.

Shakespeare's plays. But the prize exhibits are missing: no detailed drawings of the exterior have been found; cartographer's sketches of the period are disparate and short on particulars; there are no known drawings made from inside the theater; the builder's plans have been lost; and the Globe itself has been lost twice.

The first destruction of the Globe was by fire in 1613. One contemporary account puts it this way:

> Upon St. Peter's Day last, the playhouse or theatre called the Globe, upon Bankside, near London, by negligent discharge of a peal of ordnance close to the south side thereof, the thatch took fire, and the wind suddenly dispersed the flames round about, and in a very short space the whole building was quite consumed; and no man hurt: the house being filled with people to behold the play, viz. of Henry the Eight.

(Below) Witchcraft was amusing to some but serious business to most in the sixteenth and seventeenth centuries. It was a particular interest of King James I, in whose court some of Shakespeare's later plays were presented. When witches appeared in plays at the Globe, there were believers in the audience to whom the drama must have seemed terrifyingly real. (Left) A prototype Merchant of Venice is portrayed in a sixteenth century woodcut.

By this time, the Globe's owners were the wealthiest actors in London, so they had no trouble financing its reconstruction in even grander style. The second Globe lasted three decades, then withered under the frown of a hostile Puritan Parliament. All playhouses were closed by law in 1642—twenty-six years after Shakespeare's death—and the Globe was soon torn down.

Following generations showed recurrent interest in Shakespeare's plays and poems but little in his theater. In 1833, near the end of the Romantic Period in literature, the *Penny Magazine* of London paused briefly to recall the Globe in a badly muddled reminiscence and to mention that its site was then occupied by a brewery. From that time through the Victorian period, the *London Quarterly Review* pub-

lished dozens of essays on Shakespeare's works but not one speculation about the Globe. Modern scholarship has repaired part of this lapse; but to this day no one has precise knowledge of the Globe's design, and many historians believe that no one will ever know—that no decisive piece of evidence is likely to turn up.

If it did—if, miraculously, Peter Street's plans were unearthed—they might furnish structural specifics like these, taken from surviving plans for the Hope theater, drawn up in the same year that the Globe burned:

Make the principalls and fore front of the saide plaie house of good and sufficient oken tymber, and no furr tymber to be putt or used in the lower most, or midell stories, excepte the upright postes on the backparte of the said stories. (All the byndinge joystes to be of oken tymber.)

Photos, by permission of the Folger Shakespeare Library, Washington, D.C.

163

And they might supply some interior detail, as does this excerpt from an agreement for construction of the Fortune:

> All the princypall and maine postes of the saide fframe and stadge forwarde shalbe square and wroughte palasterwise with carved proporcions called Satiers to be placed & sett on the topp of every of the same postes.

It's generally assumed that the Hope was smaller than the Globe and differed considerably in design. The Fortune was large but rectangular; the Globe was octagonal. Or was it cylindrical? No doubt its basic shape was the same as that of its antecedent, The Theatre (since the same timbers were used); and the design of The Theatre was copied from the bear-baiting arenas south of the Thames. Or was it an elaboration of the inn yards on Gracious street? Or a futher development of the outdoor stage at Ghent? Or an original architectural species? Or a child of Renaissance theaters in Italy and France? Or could it be that James Burbage had direct knowledge of the Latin treatise by Vitruvius on Classical theater design? All of these possibilities have been seriously advanced and seriously challenged.

It seems fairly well established that both The Theatre and the Globe had a central yard, unroofed and surrounded by three tiers of roofed galleries, a stage that extended into the yard, a structure above the stage for machinery, and "tiring house" quarters behind the stage for dressing rooms and storage of costumes and props.

The overhead structure was referred to as The Heavens, and its underside apparently was painted with suitable celestial symbols. Machinery included a hoist to lower gods, goddesses, ghosts, or whatever figures might properly descend from heavens. For the lower end of the supernatural spectrum, there were trapdoors in the stage, out of which devils could emerge to appropriate hissing and occasional

"The Heavens" of the Globe as seen from above (left) and from the underside (facing page), as reconstructed by Dr. Adams. Inscribed with the Zodiac, the Heavens had trap doors through which to lower special props or spirits or to operate unusual lighting or sound effects. The huts on top contained bells, hoists, and other stage machinery for all this.

The theater in the Folger Shakespeare Library is patterned after Elizabethan theater designs though not the Globe itself. The plan here is rectangular instead of octagonal, and seating has been added in the "courtyard" area. In Stratford, Ontario, the renowned Festival Theater uses the octagonal form but substitutes tiered seating in the courtyard and makes the aisles serve as supplementary stage entrances.

fireworks. There was little use of painted scenery but heavy use of decoration. By some accounts the wooden columns in the Globe were painted to resemble marble and the stage area was brightly painted and festooned with garlands, tapestries, and banners. The audiences loved bright colors, rich costumes, spectacular scenes, and special effects.

There is considerable evidence that the elaborate design and paraphernalia of the stage was by no means equalled in the accommodations for playgoers. Although seating estimates vary widely, it seems likely that most of the audience at any well-attended play was crammed in on hard gallery steps with no backrests, much less armrests, while the groundlings in the central court were "closely pes-

tered together" under the afternoon sun. (Estimates of space per person vary from fourteen to twenty-two inches in seating width and from twenty to thirty inches in depth, with something between one-and-one-half and three square feet per person for standing room in the yard.) More expensive seating flanking the stage may have been more commodious, with rush matting on some of the benches. At any rate, these seats were in the shade, while many spectators in the penny galleries opposite the stage had the sun in their eyes.

Probably the best and most thoroughly detailed reconstruction of the Globe was researched and built in miniature at Hoffstra University by John Cranford Adams, author of *The Globe Playhouse: Its Design and Construction*,

166

The Bettmann Archive

assisted by Irwin Smith. This model is now exhibited at the Folger Shakespeare Library in Washington, D. C.

Down the hall in the Folger is an actual theater, designed to the general plan of Elizabethan stages if not specifically to that of the Globe. And in various cities across the United States, in Canada, and in England, there are "Elizabethan" playhouses that, to one degree or another, evoke the balconied thrust stages, encircling seats, and some of the production features of the Globe, the Swan, and the Hope, not to mention some of the plays.

If "the great globe itself" has indeed dissolved, it is not without leaving a track behind. And aside from authenticity, there are creature comforts to think about. The creatures who pay for the tickets at Stratford—Connecticut, Ontario, or England—expect not only a good production but also softer, roomier seats than their Elizabethan counterparts, in houses better sheltered from sun and rain, in which there are no groundlings "closely pestered together" and no one has to stand.

JERICHO

Why did the walls come tumbling down?

Two million years before anyone started to count, something shifted in the Earth's crust and a long, narrow slice of the surface dropped a half mile straight down, leaving a scar which now contains the Jordan River valley, the Dead sea, part of the Red sea, the Gulf of Aqaba, and the Great Rift valley through East Africa.

As seen through the lens of twentieth-century hindsight, this massive fracture has been seething ever since with upheavals of one kind or another: geological, glacial, climatic, cultural, and military.

"And the Lord said to Joshua, 'Seven priests shall bear seven trumpets of ram's horns before the Ark; and on the seventh day you shall march around the city seven times, the priests blowing their trumpets. . . . As soon as you hear the sound of the trumpet, then all the people shall shout with a great shout.'" (Josh. vi:4–5)

Culver Pictures

Ice age followed ice age, and while northern latitudes were locked in glaciation, stretches of the Middle East that are now all dust and desert became lands of perpetual rain—the sort of place where a man might be tempted to build an ark. When the last ice age—or if not the last, at least the latest—receded some 10,000 to 12,000 years ago, it left a fertile region, including an abundant freshwater spring a few miles northwest of the Dead sea.

Around this spring a stone-age settlement appeared, and around the settlement—a wall.

What the original inhabitants called their town, we don't know (probably not Prepottery Neolithic A, which is what archaeologists call it). When Joshua arrived with his army around 1300 B.C., it was named Jericho, and it was already more than twice as ancient as Rome is now. At 825 feet below sea level it is one of the lowest towns in the world, and so far as modern archaeology can determine, it could also be the oldest.

Theories of collapse

What Joshua did to Jericho is well known. Exactly how he managed to do it may never be known, but there are clues enough to tempt the imagination.

Most familiar, of course, is the "Trumpet Theory." Less familiar—since artists have ignored it and it has never been set to music—there is a "Strumpet Theory." Both have ample support in the Old Testament, which also leaves room for the most common physical explanations of the wall's collapse: an earthquake, or the simple persistence of ditchdiggers.

Other scenarios picture a demoralized townspeople huddled within a shaky, ready-to-tumble wall which was so unstable that the vibrations of ram's-horn trumpets and massed shouting were enough to unseat it. Or they suggest that a wall designed merely to stymie foot soldiers would not necessarily be sturdy

"On that day the Lord exalted Joshua in the sight of all Israel; and they stood in awe of him, as they had stood in awe of Moses." (Josh. iv:14)

enough to support the entire population of the city if they happened to crowd onto one section of its rim to glimpse the eerie processional of warriors and priests assembling outside to call awesome powers down upon their heads.

Inevitably there have also been more bizarre suggestions—of subsonic vibrations, of laser beams supplied by extraplanetary visitors—on which the scriptures offer no comment. But, as Will Durant has observed, history is so indifferently rich that it will furnish ample evidence to support almost any theory whatever.

Why Jericho?

While the walls stood, they were formidable. The odds against Joshua must have seemed long. Remnants show that Jericho's fortifications during this period included double walls, one of them twelve to fourteen feet thick. Houses in the town leaned against it, and at least one family lived inside the wall itself.

But however impregnable those defenses appeared, Joshua must have known something

The defenses Joshua had to breach at Jericho consisted of an outer wall six feet thick and an inner wall twelve to fourteen feet thick. The city had one watchtower at the northwest corner and a gate along the east side. But Joshua's forces first had to cross the Jordan river (bottom, left): "The feet of the priests bearing the Ark were dipped in the brink of the water, . . . the waters coming down from above stood and rose up in a heap far off, . . . and the people passed over opposite Jericho." (Josh. iii:15–16) To memorialize this occasion (bottom, right), "The men of Israel . . . took up twelve stones out of the midst of the Jordan, . . . and they carried them over with them to the place where they lodged, and laid them down there." (Josh. iv:8)

Outer wall in Joshua's time

Inner wall in Joshua's time

Late Bronze Age structures (c1600–1400 BC)

Recent excavations

Remnants of earlier walls

Probable course of earlier walls

Middle Bronze Age structures (c2000–1800 BC)

that gave him confidence. He knew about the walls. He knew about the town. He had sent spies who spent several days scouting it thoroughly, inside and out.

There were other cities that could have been attacked first, and a first success was imperative in the Israelites' conquest of the Promised Land. Joshua was far too astute a general to risk a costly, time-consuming failure; and yet, it was Jericho that he singled out for a siege.

What was Joshua's secret?

The first part of his secret was no secret at all but an obvious quandary. Joshua knew that somewhere, somehow, his army would have to breach its first wall. The land of Canaan was flowing not only with milk and honey but also with the migrations of nomadic tribes and with commerce between Mesopotamia and the Mediterranean ports. Its settlements had pros-

Photographic Archive of the Jewish Theological Seminary of America, New York

"So the people shouted, and the trumpets were blown. . . . And the wall fell down flat." (Josh. vi:20)

pered and become inviting targets for raids by neighboring city-states and by nomads from the south and east. So virtually every town of any consequence had a wall—or two walls, or three.

A world of walls

At every strategic point the Promised Land and all the lands around it were controlled by key cities, and the cities were secured by walls.

Though the region is sparsely supplied with quarry stone, the Sumerians had invented the brick mold about 3000 B.C., and wall building soon proliferated. Mud bricks could be made quickly and replaced quickly. Kiln-fired bricks were a luxury because combustibles were also scarce, but the bricks could be baked hard in the sun in a few weeks or, even better, a few years.

These replaced the unstable hand-packed planoconvex or "hogback" bricks of earlier structures at Jericho and elsewhere. By Joshua's time three successive civilizations had built and rebuilt at least seventeen walls around Jericho, each felled in turn by earth tremors, invaders, or gradual capitulation to sun, wind, and rain.

To the immediate west, the city of Ai was girded by a *triple* wall (which Joshua later penetrated by a ruse—pretending to retreat in panic but leaving a hidden contingent to enter the city after the Canaanite troops came charging out in pursuit). To the north Hazor was encircled by a 24-foot-thick brick wall on stone foundations. Gibeon, Megiddo, and Hebron had walls. Jerusalem, though most of its now-familiar structures had yet to be built, was so strongly fortified that Joshua simply skipped it in the conquest of Canaan. It remained defiantly Canaanite until the time of David, some 300 years later.

Had the Israelites ranged beyond the land of Canaan, their odds would have grown even worse. To the east lay the city of Ur, birthplace of Abraham, at the junction of the Tigris and Euphrates, where an enormous elliptical wall of baked brick stood on a rampart of unbaked brick seventy-seven feet thick. Around Ur's sister city, Uruk, a six-mile wall was studded with 900 defense towers (Jericho had one).

On the east bank of the Tigris, Nineveh would eventually surpass even this, with King Sennacherib's seven-mile perimeter of quadruple walls, fifteen gates, 1,500 watchtowers, and a 130-foot-wide moat surrounding it all. The Greek historian Diodorus claimed (though other historians doubt) that these walls were 100 feet high and the towers 214 feet high.

Nebuchadnezzar's Babylon flourished behind *five* concentric rings of fortifications, and the inner two were filled in between with rubble to form a combined wall eighty-eight feet thick. By the time the Babylonians added moats and crenelated parapets to this system, there was no practical way to gain entry except to go to the Ishtar gate and bribe someone.

Jericho's defenses had achieved no such splendor. Two or three foundation courses of stone were topped by rough courses of mud brick, backed by an interior facing of packed clay. There was an outer wall, six feet thick, and an inner wall roughly twice as massive. The twelve to eighteen feet between the two was open except at the northwest corner, where it was filled in to support a forty-foot watchtower.

Inside the walls

But there was something else between those walls. An accomplice. Her name was Rahab, her profession as old as the town itself; and she and her family were destined to be the only survivors of Jericho after the fall.

When Joshua had sent two of his men to

scout the defenses of Jericho, it was Rahab they had visited.

"All who live in this territory have been seized with terror at your approach," she told them, "for we have heard how Yahweh dried up the Sea of Reeds before you when you came out of Egypt. . . . No courage is left in any of us to stand up to you."

These were the Canaanites, part of the Phoenician civilization, and the people who would later build Carthage and very nearly conquer Rome. But it was the Canaanites a thousand years before Hannibal, and there was no such able general to oppose Joshua or to rally the townspeople.

When word spread through the security-conscious town that there were two outsiders in Rahab's house, she hid them under a pile of flax stalks on her roof and claimed they had already left. Later she helped them to escape in exchange for the promise that her family would be spared when Jericho was overrun.

Three days later the spies returned to the Israelite encampment at nearby Gilgal. On hearing their story, Joshua immediately struck camp and marched on Jericho.

Outside the walls

The odds were improving. A frightened populace, roughly 2,000 people, were apparently huddled in their eight-acre enclosure, convinced they were doomed.

Still, there were the walls.

After six days of siege nothing appeared to have changed, and the fortifications stood firm. It's possible that an earthquake on the seventh day broke the stalemate: a theory often advanced, and a credible one in view of the region's history of seismic surprises. Its timing, however, would indeed be miraculous if the walls were to collapse on cue. More plausibly, the Israelites might have arrived just after a fortuitous earthquake had left Jericho defenseless, in which case the Book of Joshua would have to be seen as a narrative stretched to glorify one of the founding fathers.

But what keeps surprising secular scholars of history and archaeology is the remarkable extent to which the Old Testament holds up, verified by other evidence time after time, as a reliable reflection of history. If the scriptures say Joshua's army circled the town and his priests blew their rams' horns and the wall fell, then that may be precisely what happened. And Rahab may be the *reason* it happened.

The art of sapping was not unknown, and Joshua would have come prepared to have his own ditchdiggers undermine the fortifications if there were any means of getting them close enough to do it.

One means would be to have some of them inside, say, in Rahab's house. Another would be to distract the defenders so effectively that the sappers could work unnoticed from the outside, or at least enter unnoticed and then go to work digging between the inner and the outer walls to undermine both.

An opening for surreptitious entry is suggested by one quirk of construction in several generations of the Jericho walls. They were sometimes rebuilt in sections, with narrow spaces left between sections, apparently to localize damage when one portion collapsed. It is not known whether Jericho's seventeenth wall had this feature but, if so, a compelling diversion on one side of the city might be more than enough to permit entry through crevices on the opposite side. And there is mention in the Book of Joshua that Rahab had agreed to hang a scarlet cord outside the wall to mark her residence.

As for diverting the attention of the defenders, Joshua had worked out one of the most elaborate distractions in the history of psychological warfare.

Six times, once each day, his army marched in solemn and silent procession around the city, accompanied by seven priests carrying

"Then they utterly destroyed all in the city, both men and women, young and old, oxen, sheep, and asses, with the edge of the sword." (Josh. vi:21)

trumpets and others bearing the Ark of the Covenant. One can imagine the cumulative terror of the people inside as they beheld what Isaac Asimov has called "the somber and majestic spinning of a supernatural net about the city."

On the seventh day, the procession began early and did not cease until it had circled the city seven times. Then it stopped. Silence, followed by the sudden blare of trumpets and a mighty shout from the whole Israelite army.

When they heard the sound of the trumpet, the people raised a mighty war cry, and the wall collapsed then and there.

The Israelites stormed the town, destroyed it, and killed everyone in it except Rahab and her family. Joshua decreed that Jericho should never be rebuilt, and he backed up the decree with a curse:

Cursed be the man before the Lord, that riseth up and buildeth this city, Jericho.

Curses last longer than walls.

The Israelites kept their distance from the blighted site. When they finally rebuilt Jericho, 400 years later, it was nearly two miles from the first location. This in turn was leveled during the Roman occupation, about the time of Christ. Herod sacked the city, then built it up again to include a palace. Persian invaders destroyed that. The Crusaders built yet another Jericho, this time a mile downstream from the water supply, and theirs was obliterated by Saladin. The present-day town is next to the original, still using the same freshwater spring; but the Jericho flattened by Joshua is still flat.

Nothing remains but a broad mound of rubble, a compost heap of human events where archaeologists carve careful trenches, meticulously sorting out what happened, and in what order, after the first known instance in all of history when it occurred to someone to build a wall.

THE FALLEN IDOL

Monumental sculptures of Rhodes

In his search for building materials, man has used snow, grass, basalt, mud, paper, and pelts. But never has there been a procurement effort quite like the mustering of construction materials that took place around 300 B.C. in the city of Rhodes.

To defend their island against imminent siege, the citizens of Rhodes tore down some of their best architecture and converted the rubble into massive battlements. Two years later, when the battle was won, they reversed the process: they dismantled the attacker's catapults and siege machines and used the metal, plus some of the stone from their own ramparts, to erect their celebrated war memorial, the Colossus of Rhodes. The cycle was to renew itself

COLOSSVS SOLIS.

History's second-largest colossus stood for 56 years, and its legends have grown for 2,200 years since its collapse. It stood beside the harbor of Rhodes, not astride its entrance as often depicted. The largest colossus ever built is still standing—in New York Harbor—at roughly twice the height.

179

nine centuries later, when the Saracens sold what was left of the Colossus for scrap metal—to be used for weapons.

A colossal threat

Rhodes, in the era of its Colossus, was one of the world's most beautiful, most civilized cities. Politically it had outgrown the leadership of Athens and had become an ally of Ptolemy's Egypt, at the expense of a former partner, Macedonia. Demetrius Poliorcetes of Macedonia decided to retaliate, and mounted a punitive expedition whose army of 40,000 outnumbered the entire population of Rhodes.

When the Rhodians heard of the invasion plan, they began to fortify the island. Very few stones were left unturned.

They tore down temples—many temples, because the early Rhodians had recognized many deities. They added the stone and marble to their rising battlements and melted the metal to forge weapons. And they sacrificed much of the city's magnificent public works for defense: ripping out walls for their stone, sealing off roads with fortifications, and closing down one of the busiest harbors of the ancient world.

Rhodes executed one of the most thorough mobilization plans in history. Every man, wom-

The Bettmann Archive, Inc.

Designed by the famed sculptor Chares, the Colossus was a monument to Helios and a celebration of victory over the Macedonians.

an, and child trained for the battle. Even cripples had their wartime assignments, and slaves were promised their freedom if they would fight alongside their masters.

The siege lasted over a year. Though plague-ridden and close to starvation, the Rhodians held out until a rescue fleet from Ptolemy forced the Macedonians into hurried retreat—so hurried that they left most of their formidable arsenal of war machines behind.

A monumental triumph

Leaders of Rhodes decided that Macedonian siege weapons would make an excellent monu-

ment to Macedonian defeat. They commissioned the great sculptor-architect Chares to design a colossal monument to the sun god Helios (the Rhodian counterpart of Apollo) while some of his fellow citizens set to work extracting his building materials from the remnants of war.

Bronze, by this time, had come into its own. Techniques of hollow casting had arrived from Egypt or Assyria, and the metal was widely used in the sculpture of Greece and Samos. In monumental architecture, bronze was prized not only for its beauty but for its permanence, its natural corrosion resistance. By the time Chares was ready with his design, his salvage

181

Was the Colossus a lighthouse as well as a monument? By day, its bronze skin would reflect sunlight far out to sea. Although many accounts tell of a torch held aloft, it is not certain that there was any method for keeping it ablaze through the night.

COLOSSUS SOLIS

The Bettmann Archive, Inc.

crews were ready with 500 talents of bronze (nearly 30,000 pounds) and 300 talents of iron.

Chares' plan was a daring one. The pedestal alone would stand higher than most statues known at the time — 45 feet, all of white marble.

The Colossus would tower another 105 feet skyward, to a total height of 150 feet.

The Colossus was built in sections, each partially assembled on the ground and then raised into place with the aid of wooden scaffolding. It had a skin of bronze, hammered so thin that in finished form the outer shell was no thicker than a penny.

For structural strength Chares designed an iron skeleton inside the hollow bronze form, and a huge external brace hidden by the cape of the Colossus. For further stability each section of the hollow legs was filled with stone as soon as it was in place. (Postwar Rhodes could now reconvert its stone fortifications to peacetime public works.)

Chares built a model of each piece before

the bronze part was made. Then workmen would copy his miniature. The most highly skilled craftsmen on the island supervised this work, then personally did the final metalworking for each part.

What went wrong?

At least two historians who later visited the site—Pliny and Phylon—regarded the Colossus as the most perfect execution of the human form they had ever seen. Its architect was less satisfied. Chares committed suicide before the Colossus was finished, and his work had to be completed by Laches.

Accounts differ as to why Chares killed himself, but apparently his reason was one of two common frustrations of architects in all ages. One version has it that Chares had become disconsolate over some flaw in the design. The other is that he thought he had lost face when it became apparent that the costs of the project would be substantially more colossal than his original estimates.

The second version has certain earmarks of a history written by an architect, but it should be remembered that the Rhodians had good reason to expect that the estimate would be accurate. The Colossus of Rhodes was only one—albeit the largest and best one—of rough-

Felled by an earth tremor, the colossal sculpture which had stood for half a century now lay for nine centuries on the ground. Its metal pieces were last seen headed for the Turkish mainland in the year 653, for remelting. Perhaps in a museum case somewhere is a last, unrecognizable remnant, in the form of a Saracen sword.

ly a hundred "colossal" statues that populated the island.

There have been many accounts of the final form and function of the Colossus. Some are clearly apocryphal, such as the legend that it stood astride the harbor, with ships coming and going between its legs. Some controversies have yet to be settled—for example, the argument as to whether the Colossus held a harbor light aloft.

The fallen idol

The reason for this uncertainty, and for the scarcity of good descriptions of the Colossus, is that it stood for only fifty-six years before it was felled by an earthquake. It was in this prone and fragmented condition that most chroniclers saw it before writing their accounts.

Pliny reported: "Few men can clasp the thumb in their arms, and its fingers are larger than most statues."

Hardly a century went by without at least one attempt to raise the fallen idol, but all efforts failed. Finally, in A.D. 653, the Saracens carted off the remains—by merchant fleet to the mainland, then inland on the backs of 950 camels—for reconversion into weapons.